For Julian,
and for Jane.

Contents

Foreword

by Lynne Truss

At a multi-author Christmas bookshop event in London in 2003, I met a woman who said she despaired of ever learning the rules of punctuation. Since I was sitting at a signing desk at the time, with a pile of *Eats, Shoots & Leaves* in front of me, I naturally wondered whether she was winding me up on purpose. But apparently not. 'Oh, punctuation, punctuation,' she moaned. (To be fair, she did look tired.) 'There's just no help to be found, is there? Commas, semicolons, apostrophes. I mean, once you've passed a certain point in your education, there's just *no way* you can go back and learn how to use an apostrophe. It's a closed book *for ever*.'

Composing my face into a sunny salesgirl smile, I held up a copy of my (then) bestselling book on punctuation at a jaunty angle, and cocked an eyebrow – but she didn't take the hint. 'And I'm a teacher!' she went on. 'An English teacher! So I *know* there's just nothing to be done, not once you've passed a certain point in your education; nothing to be done; nothing to be done ...' And then she walked away. I don't know whose desk she arrived at next, but I like to think of her stopping to tell Delia Smith that boiling an egg was a mysterious operation that could never be learned later in life, either. ('And I'm a chef! A chef at the Savoy!')

Why have I remembered this defeatist woman all these years? I mean, apart from the horrific detail that she was an English teacher? Well, partly because I did understand what she meant about missed opportunities. There is a moment, isn't there, when you get a new household gadget and you promise yourself – you absolutely promise yourself – that you really will sit down with the manual this time, and find out what this thing can do. But then, once you've used it a couple of times to do baked potatoes (I'm thinking microwave ovens here), you forget all about the great earnest learning project, and the manual ends up in an obscure kitchen drawer along with some rusty old secateurs and a ball of string, to be found by the house-clearers after your death.

It's the same with anything technical. I've had my current car for six months, and driven about five thousand miles in it, and I realised a couple of days ago that I still have only a vague notion of how to put the lights on full beam. Since there has been no reason to open the bonnet yet, I have no idea how to do that, either. More important, I suspect, is the choice of drive modes (it's an automatic). It shames me to admit this, but I can't remember what the difference is. So sometimes I put it in 'S' (which I think stands for 'Sporty', but it could be 'Shopping') and sometimes I put it in the other one, in case I've been missing something by selecting 'S'. The point I am making here is that, basically, it is human nature to skip the learning part, and get straight to the motorway-driving – to be content to pick up the details on the hoof later, or maybe not pick them up at all. Which is what I shall feebly say in my defence, of course, when one day I enter a darkened tunnel and crash immediately, because I never learned how to locate those pesky lights.

The good news is that writing without understanding the rules of punctuation rarely leads to actual loss of life. The bad news is that the bookshop woman is not alone in feeling that she's all at sea, punctuation-wise, having missed out on learning something fundamental about written language – something that could still help her, not just occasionally, but every day. Writing is what we mainly do with our time nowadays, surely. We write almost incessantly. We live in a mass-communicating world in which writing is the key life skill. So, what a tragedy that so many people haven't been taught how to do it – having been told instead (in school) that writing was a joyful self-expression kind of thing, completely removed from horrible Victorian ideas of getting marked down in red pen for 'mistakes'. The orthodox notion appears to have been: what does it matter if we turn out people who are technically illiterate and therefore unemployable, just as long as they think they are expressing themselves, and don't associate the act of writing with getting things 'wrong', which is so bad for self-esteem?

The irony is that, years ago, when most people *did* know how to write, they mostly didn't have to. Just twenty years ago, even in newspaper offices, people didn't write much at all. Typewriters were not to be found on every desk. In fact, typing was a job done, in those days, almost exclusively by secretaries: under-paid and overlooked women who had been trained in chalky school-rooms (with ticking metronomes) to type at a monitored speed, to lay out letters correctly, to check word spellings in dictionaries, and to amend the grammar of their better-paid superiors. In the world of work, people were generally not bent silently over keyboards all day. They were noisily on the phone, or drilling into a seam of coal, or screwing bits onto car doors, or dealing with customers face-to-face. As for young people, writing letters in their bedrooms was the last thing they wanted to do. They played outside with their friends, and kept alive lovely olde-worlde childhood traditions, like cat's cradle, and hopscotch, and arson.

But now we write, write, write. In just a couple of decades, the proliferation of texting, emailing and social networking means that most of us spend most of our leisure time as well as our work time composing, sending, and receiving written messages. Increasingly, we represent ourselves to others by the way we write! So it's a very exposing time for people who missed out on some useful first principles. Personally, I think it's a wonderful time for the written word: I love the fact that we can communicate with other people – instantly – wherever we are and whatever else we're doing. Truly, if Apple invented a bath sponge with a keyboard in it, I would be among the ten million people queuing up to buy one on launch day. But there is a downside. Evidently, when many people look at the colon, the dash, and the semicolon on their keyboards, they don't immediately see in them an opportunity to express complex thoughts in longer sentences. What they tend to see, primarily, is a pair of eyes, on its side; a long, straight nose, on its side; and a pair of eyes, with one of them winking, on its side.

Anyway, you guessed where this was all leading. This terrific workbook, *Can You Eat, Shoot & Leave?*, is what that poor bookshop woman knew that she needed; it is the missing manual to end all missing manuals. It is full of cunning exercises designed to teach all the ways in which the much-misunderstood comma, apostrophe, bracket and hyphen can organise words into sensible groups, clarify meaning, and generally bring order out of chaos. I'm so glad it supports the apostrophe, even though it's a lost cause. Over the past few years, I have heard many people say that the apostrophe 'complicates things'. Well, call me an old romantic, but when I have heard them say this, I have wanted to punch them in the face. The apostrophe is a harmless, helpful, elegant little mark which, admittedly, has taken on rather too many jobs for its own good, but should never be blamed for the fact that, in English, words end in 's' for a variety of reasons. It is *English* that is complicated, not the apostrophe. Of course, usage is shifting at a great speed, and the apostrophe's days are definitely numbered. It is quickly disappearing from signs. In its death throes, it is responsible for quite funny mistakes such as:

SPOIL YOUR LOVED ONE'S
VALENTINES DAY, FEBRUARY 14

But it has done its job beautifully for centuries, and I just won't stand for it to be insulted.

The two things I love most about this book are that: a) it requires you to pick up a pencil, sharpen it, and make marks; and b) it doesn't expect you to know much about grammar. In other words, it takes an entirely practical approach – which is what I was striving for myself in *Eats, Shoots & Leaves*, having personally come from a background in editing, not linguistics. After university, my first proper job was editing book reviews for an academic weekly newspaper (the *Times Higher Education Supplement*), and it was there, at age 22, that I pored over the *Times* style book, and marvelled at the significant difference in meaning between words such as 'continuous' and 'continual', or 'masterful' and 'masterly'. I memorised *Times* style for words such as 'judgment' and 'Dostoevsky'. I finally sorted out 'practise' and 'practice'. My boss had a personal *bête noire:* the verb 'stress', she said, pertained only to the world of engineering (editors always have these idiosyncrasies). So unless the context was concrete (*stressed* concrete), we always took it out.

Looking back, I can't help feeling we were pretty savage and arbitrary editors, my boss and I. We tore into manuscripts, covering them with deletions, transpositions, and insertions. In fact, we often got so carried away with all our inky marks that we had to get a clean copy of the offending original from the filing cabinet, and go at it vigorously afresh. In those days, we used to send galley proofs back to the reviewers, and I can now only imagine the shock and hurt we inflicted. 'I didn't write *this*! I didn't write anything *like* this!' those poor academics must have said. 'And why have they changed "stress" to "emphasise"? That's the final straw!' But it wasn't all one-way, by any means: I was often on the receiving end of brutal, no-nonsense newspaper editing myself. I remember the dispiriting occasion when I delivered a theatre review in person to an editor at the *Times Literary Supplement*; without first reading it through, he just started at the top and

– reading as he went – steadily crossed it out in front of me, line by line, in thick black pencil ('*This* can go; don't need *this*; nope, don't need *this*,') until he finally reached a bit he liked. 'Here we are,' he said, stopping the crossing-out half-way through the second paragraph and making a mark. 'We'll start here.'

The whole point of writing is to transmit a thought from your own mind to someone else's as clearly and efficiently as possible. You know how in *The Highway Code* it says you should never cause another motorist to swerve or brake or stop? It's the same with writing. Don't make your reader screech to a halt in confusion, or take an abrupt left into a ditch. In my opinion, it really helps if you have a tiny Editor Within who stands back from the words and spots where the collisions are likely to happen: 'Would this sentence work better the other way round? Is that comma misleading? Is "bastard" the right word here? If that's a whole sentence, why isn't there a full stop at the end?' This Editor Within doesn't have to make you cry; it doesn't have to rip out all your jokes, leaving tender, traumatised, joke-shaped holes; or insist that you can't start a sentence with the word 'And' (apparently it's against the law, but I take no notice). It's all about common sense and paying attention, really; just remembering that the person to whom you are transmitting your thoughts has nothing else to go on but the words you have provided – with punctuation marks for that crucial extra guidance. An Editor Within is a true friend, and the reason I applaud this terrific book is that I believe it will provide you with an Editor Within. You will never be at sea, punctuation-wise, again.

Who Do You Think You Are?

In its scrutiny of what's going wrong in present-day punctuation of the English language, Lynne Truss's *Eats, Shoots and Leaves* declared war on grammatical indifference. Her book was a battle-cry to sticklers everywhere and made millions of people look twice at the marks they were (or weren't) making on a page. Humbly treading where Lynne Truss has gone before, in this workbook I aim to provide not only sticklers but anyone who's interested with a thorough understanding of the rules of punctuation. I also hope that, on the way, we might just gain a sense of wonder about punctuation and its place in our language, for it is that wonder which will ultimately see us right.

Now here's the question; why are *you* here? Perhaps you suffer mild chest pain at a glimpse of an ill-placed apostrophe? Do you suspect there's a difference between a colon and a semicolon but would rather not be asked exactly what, thanks? Or are you, quite frankly, bewildered by the punctuation that you see around you? No matter where you come in that list there is one thing about you that I already know, beyond doubt: you care. Good on you, and welcome to the club. Ours is not an exclusive society, I'm afraid. Quite the opposite: we are striving to include anyone with even a passing interest in improving their punctuation. I am not an academic, nor am I a grammarian. I am just another (albeit fairly obsessive) punter who happens to like language, tries to write what I mean and tries to use punctuation to the best of my knowledge to make my point. On top of that, however, I believe that everyone can and should have a basic aptitude for punctuation at their fingertips, without effort, and – perhaps most importantly – without anxiety.

There is no doubt at all that many of the functions of punctuation have already been eroded by our carelessness. What we see as 'mistakes' today will become the standard usage of tomorrow. Such is the way of things; without change like this we would not speak or write the English we do now. Well in that case, I hear you cry, aren't we, by learning and enforcing the current rules of punctuation, standing in the way of what is a natural and worthwhile process of change? Well, I don't think so. Having a sound comprehension of punctuation makes us trustworthy judges of those instances when rule-breaking or changing patterns of usage add value, or take it away; whether they make written English communicate better, worse, or are simply mistakes; whether they should be embraced, or resisted at all costs. Consider an example, the likes of which we have all seen a million times:

Thank you for your confirmation. Your four candle's are on there way to you.

Blunders like these make me fear for our children (pain mitigated only by the distant echo of the classic Four Candles sketch from *The Two Ronnies*). As is so often the way, the email that contained two such howlers was otherwise carefully presented – if you like that sort of thing – in a quaint typeface with a delicate background of pale pastels. But, pretty as it was, the missive was rendered near meaningless by its core mistakes. Why make all that (misguided) effort in one respect yet forego basic correctness? The Scottish saying 'all fur coat and nae knickers' comes to mind. It is *this* abuse of punctuation that we must oppose at all costs, for it comes not from a conscious and intelligent decision to create an effect, nor from a valuable drift in common usage; it is merely careless, confused, and unhelpful.

While I neither expect nor hope that we punctuate perfectly in our texts, emails and tweets, I do believe that we should be able to shift up a couple of punctuation gears when the time is right. By all means, skip the odd apostrophe while battering off a quick message. But shouldn't we retain, at the other end of the spectrum, our ability to compose a flawless cover letter that secures a life-changing job, or a plea so beautifully crafted that it will win back the heart of a lover? This is what I hope for us: competence in punctuation not for competence's sake, but for the sake of communicating – without undermining errors – our most human voices.

We are here to learn, but more importantly, to have a bit of fun while doing so. If at any point you need to restore a little perspective (which you probably inherently lack, seeing as you already worry about little typographical marks), take yourself off to find some archive footage of Danish comedian (and pianist) Victor Borge's famous 'Phonetic Punctuation' routine. There is one particularly sparkling performance alongside Dean Martin, who is smoking a cigarette on stage – oh, those heady days! It's a peach, and a worthwhile reminder not to take things too seriously. Learning is brilliant. Language is funny. Punctuation, in both the right and the wrong hands, can be downright hilarious.

Enough already. Let's start our journey by finding out where you are on the punctuation compass. Everyone is welcome – from novice to expert – especially those with pencils at the ready.

A little punctuation initiation

1   It's Saturday lunch time; you are in town and starving. You pass a placard for the local deli, promising 'a huge range of hot and cold sandwich's, panini's to take away'. Do you:

   A   Step right in while straightening out the fiver from your pocket?
   B   Wince quietly at the mistreatment of the apostrophes, but linger to peruse the menu?
   C   Lose your appetite, whip out a marker pen and correct the two plurals just before the deli owner smacks your fingers away from replacing the comma with *and*?

2   Which one of the following is correct?

   The three girl's handbag's were locked in the nightclubs cloakrooms.

   The three girls' handbags were locked in the nightclub's cloakrooms.

   A   The first one.

B The second one.

C You couldn't possibly answer until it is made totally and incontrovertibly clear whether there was one nightclub with several cloakrooms, or whether there were indeed three nightclubs, with a cloakroom in each.

3 **On entering a rather lovely public park with Fritz, your miniature Schnauzer, you see a sign which reads 'No dogs please'. What do you do?**

A Think that it's a bit of a poor show and try somewhere else.

B Leave the park grudgingly while reflecting that the sign read a bit oddly.

C Mutter to yourself, 'Well actually, in my experience most of them do!'

4 **Which one of the following is correct?**

A Don't look now, but the girl, who is looking right at us, is an ex of my brother.

B Don't look now, but the girl who is looking right at us is an ex of my brother.

C Don't look now, but the girl who is looking right at us is an ex of my brother's.

5 **Your local health food café invites you to 'Go the whole hog, why not come in for camomile tea and bran muffins'. What is your reaction, apart from an involuntary gag?**

A Why isn't there a question mark at the end?

B There is definitely a question mark missing, and shouldn't there be a full stop after *hog*?

C It needs a question mark and perhaps a full stop after *hog*, but wouldn't a semicolon there be marginally better?

6   **Which one of the following is correct?**

A   He couldn't have been happier, however, he wondered why Sophie 'felt much downcast'.

B   He couldn't have been happier; however he wondered why Sophie 'felt much downcast'.

c   He couldn't have been happier; however, he wondered why Sophie 'felt much downcast.'

7   **She often wrote on her hand as an _____.**

A   *aide memoire*

B   *aide-memoire*

c   aide-memoire

8   **How might you punctuate the following sentence to best reflect this material girl's declaration?**

She vehemently declared that diamonds bright sparkling diamonds were indeed this girl's best friend.

A   She vehemently declared that diamonds, bright, sparkling diamonds, were indeed this girl's best friend.

B   She vehemently declared that diamonds (bright, sparkling diamonds) were indeed this girl's best friend.

c   She vehemently declared that diamonds – bright, sparkling diamonds – were indeed this girl's best friend.

9   **Would you add any punctuation to the following?**

He bought her a second hand washing machine for her birthday. He had always been tight fisted.

A   No, I would leave it as it is.

B   Yes, but only before *hand*: He bought her a second-hand washing machine for her birthday. He had always been tight fisted.

C   Yes; before *hand* and also before *fisted*: He bought her a second-hand washing machine for her birthday. He had always been tight-fisted.

10 You've checked into a hotel after a long drive and it's 9.00 p.m. You spot a sign that reads 'Dinner served from 6 p.m.-9.15 p.m.' Do you:

A   Chuck your bags in the room and hot-foot it to the restaurant.

B   Point out that the hyphen should actually have been a dash on their sign.

C   Waste 15 minutes, and your last chance of a hot meal, explaining what an en rule is and that the word *from* should be removed in this instance.

Surveying the damage

If you answered mostly A:

Congratulations on buying this book, for in it lies the path to enlightenment. I am afraid that punctuation is not your strong suit, is it? Don't despair, however; in no time at all we'll have you punctuating your plural possessives without a bat of your eyelids.

If you answered mostly B:

You've a dim recollection of childhood, or most likely, teen-age, grammar lessons. In fact, you were probably taught the rudiments when your exasperated French teacher discovered that you hadn't been taught any English grammar so rattled you through a crash course before he could start any French. It happened to us all. You've a good firm grasp of how punctuation works, however. By the end of this book we will have turned you into an expert.

If you answered mostly c:
Please tell me you haven't found any typos in this book yet. No, seriously, put that pencil away.

At Your Service, Master:

The Apostrophe

Consider the poor apostrophe, so eager and willing, yet so often misunderstood. What's worse, so often in the wrong place at the wrong time. The pop industry is perhaps the most visibly guilty of its maltreatment. The apostrophe was publicly ensnared in the band name Hear'Say before the group did the right thing and broke up, releasing the innocent punctuation mark. Hijacked by an Australian band in 2002 it briefly adorned the unsettling title Scandal'us. However, even they couldn't stand the guilt of its wrongful imprisonment. The ill-fated singers shuffled off shamefaced, leaving the apostrophe at the mercy of the next pop wannabe. And so it goes on.

Abuse of the apostrophe is, however, a symptom of its very character. It is obedient, enthusiastic, and capable of carrying out many important tasks. A bit like a spaniel, you might say. However that's where the analogy ends, because we are usually quite nice to spaniels.

Where did it come from?

The apostrophe first appeared in the English language in the 16th century simply to mark omitted letters. The word's Greek root means 'turn away' and from that, 'omission' or 'elision'. Always one for a new trend, Shakespeare scattered it liberally throughout his plays to carry out that duty. Later, printers began to use it to mark possessives; first singular 'the boy's hat' and then plural 'the boys' hats'. Then, as we heaped ever more responsibility onto the wide-eyed apostrophe, everything went to hell in a handcart until, now, we are guilty of putting it to work in places it just shouldn't be. Think of cafés boasting of 'Freshly ground coffee's'. Shocking brutality. End it now by reading on.

Warm-up

First up, let's just get thinking about apostrophes, with no agenda and no point-scoring.

1 **Working only on your gut instincts, rewrite the following sentences with as many apostrophes as you think could be correctly inserted:**

   For example: The four spiders webs were not as intimidating as he had thought.

   The four spiders' webs weren't as intimidating as he'd thought.

   A She did not believe that he would ever return to their houses fireside.

B He had not shown up since 1987. But if her mother said he would turn up in two weeks time, she would probably be right.

2 **Now be Eliza Doolittle for a moment. How could you make the following reflect how Eliza spoke?**

A Come on, Dover, move yer blooming arse!

B In Hertford, Hereford and Hampshire, hurricanes hardly ever happen.

Made you think? Racked your brains a bit? Smashing! That's all we wanted to achieve. Now, let's remind ourselves properly of what the apostrophe does for a living.

The apostrophe: what should we use it for?

1 *To indicate a possessive in a singular noun, or, in layman's terms, to say that one thing belongs to another:*

The president's right-hand man.

The Chamber of Commerce's red leather sofa.

When the possessor is a plural that doesn't end in 's' (an irregular plural), the apostrophe stays before the 's':

The women's magazine.

The people's vote.

The men's loo.

When the possessor is a regular plural, so ends in an 's', the apostrophe comes after that 's':

The families' welfare.

The ladies' rugby club.

The lads' night out.
Mothers' Day.

2 *To indicate time or quantity:*
A few days' holiday.
Three quid's worth.
Two weeks' notice.

A distant uncomfortable memory? Alarm bells ringing? Yup, the movie title was wrong. Wrong, wrong, wrong.

If this rule doesn't come naturally, try changing the sentence construction back to front, e.g. a holiday of a few days, a worth of three quid, a notice of two weeks. If it works and you can hear a possessive forming, then you need an apostrophe. Listen out for that 'of' whispering its presence to you.

3 *To indicate the omission of figures in dates:*
The summer of '69. (*Hear that guitar solo.*)

4 *To indicate the omission of letters:*
Exit 3 for P'wick A'port

Such contractions appear on motorway exit signs and are badly painted on the lanes of roundabouts. How do foreign tourists cope?

You're the one that I want!
They're never the same twice, my lasagnes.
I'd've gotten away with it if it weren't for you meddling kids.
Ahoy there cap'n!

Some well-established omissions no longer need an apostrophe. If, for example, you were to write in an email that you hadn't come to the 'phone because you had the 'flu, it would be forgivable to think your style a little quaint, not to say archaic. Some contractions, like 'blog' from 'weblog', have bypassed a contraction apostrophe to become new words almost immediately.

Most importantly and yet most problematically, this 'omission' function of the apostrophe creates the word 'it's'. Listen up. The word 'it's' simply means 'it is' or 'it has'. Nothing else. Simple. Don't be confused by other people getting it wrong. See the following:

It's never too late to be what you might have been.[1] (It is …)
It's as large as life, and twice as natural![2] (It is …)
It's always been a challenge, this punctuation business. (It has …)
It's never been easy to mind your p's and q's. (It has …)

If you have trouble knowing when to use 'it's', say the sentence aloud in full, using 'it is' or 'it has'. If the sentence doesn't make sense, you need the other, possessive, 'its'. Honest.

5 *To indicate non-standard English:*

'Well, here's a game!' cried Sam. 'Only think o' my master havin' the pleasure o' meeting your'n, up stairs, and me havin' the joy o' meetin' you down here. How *are* you gettin' on, and how *is* the chandlery bis'ness likely to do? …'[3]

'Oh! My lordy, lordy! *Raf* '? Dey ain' no raf' no mo', she done broke loose en gone!'[4]

Often this use of the apostrophe is tipping a wink to the reader that the character is from a social sub-class, has questionable morals, or even criminal tendencies.

6   *It appears in Irish names such as O'Sullivan and O'Connor.*

Spell such names with a comma or a hyphen at your peril. It does happen.

7   *To indicate the plural of letters when not doing so would cause significant ambiguity:*

She had dotted all her i's and crossed her t's.

He couldn't distinguish his u's from his w's.

This use of the apostrophe may feel wrong to you (especially if you are one who winces at seeing what is known as the greengrocer's apostrophe: 'pizza's made to order', 'ripe pear's half price'). However, it is preferable in those specific cases where adding an 's' to form a plural of a letter would create a word in its own right, and – hey presto – untold confusion for the reader. If more than one of these little blighters appear in quick succession (as you saw above), and one makes a word but the other doesn't, you should use an apostrophe throughout to standardise. No one – myself included – who respects punctuation likes seeing the apostrophe used here. It's not pretty, I know; but it works.

8   *To indicate the plural of words where not using it might cause confusion:*

I've had enough of your no's; please just do it.

Again, this might make your skin crawl a bit (it does mine) but leaving the above example without an apostrophe may lead the reader (or worse, the reader aloud) into a blind alley where his brain has already formed the wrong vowel sound (noss) before getting the point.

All pretty straightforward so far? Well there are some muddier waters to wade into. More on those after the exercises to follow.

The apostrophe: exercise 1

Right, it's your turn. Sharpen that HB. Defacing books, even in an intellectually legitimate way, may not come naturally to you, but marking text directly on the page may be most helpful in the long run. You'd best get used to wielding a pencil or pen over any piece of writing; you're becoming the expert, remember?

1   **Punctuate the following to indicate one singular and one plural possessive:**

There is an iron 'scolds bridle' in Walton Church. They used these things in ancient days for curbing womens tongues. They have given up the attempt now. I suppose iron was getting scarce, and nothing else would be strong enough.[5]

2   **Think about how many children are being referred to in the following (from a well-known supermarket chain). What do you think they really meant to say?**

A   Boy's toys   _____ toys

B Girl's toys   _____ toys

C Kid's DVDs   _____ DVDs[6]

3 **What is this frequently seen sign actually saying in full? And what did it mean to say?**

No dog's allowed, please.[7]

4 **Paying close attention to the context will tell you what the possessive 'number' should be in the following. Can you insert the missing apostrophe(s) in each?**

   A More than one newspaper has been ruined by the brilliant writer in the editors chair.[8]

   B A beginners guide to catching up online.

   C The lads big night out went tits up. Their two minibuses exhausts were plugged by a hen party gone bad.

   D Their horror stories similarities were remarkable.

5 **Pay close attention to number when the apostrophe denotes time and quantity:**

   A 'There she goes,' he said, 'there she goes, with two pounds worth of food on board that belongs to me, and that I haven't had.'[9]

   B In two weeks time I'll be drinking cold cider in Somerset, but I'm giving my boss not one sodding days notice.

6 **Use apostrophes to change the following sentences into more familiar sayings. Watch your number:**

   A The work of a woman is never done.

   B Let's have a drink for the sake of old times.

   C Hurry up, for the sake of Pete!

7 **Contract the following dates into more conversational English using apostrophes:**

   A The last moon landing was in the winter of 1972, the year I was born.

   B My mum wore miniskirts in the 1960s; did yours?

   C I was in the class of 1992. It was a big 'un.

8 **Add 'it's' or 'its' to the following:**

   A _____ not over 'til the fat lady sings.

   B The dog has had _____ day.

   C _____ a Wonderful Life.

   D Any colour – so long as _____ black.[10]

   E The yard was so dark that even Scrooge, who knew _____ every stone, was fain to grope with his hands.[11]

9 **Contract this into a more memorable quote from Al Harris, American football cornerback. All you need are four apostrophes and to lose a few letters:**

   'Would have, could have, should have. The bottom line is we did not do it.'

10 **Apostrophes, used correctly, are a gift to advertisers. Ignoring, for the moment, its 'inventive' lack of all other punctuation, make this former Pepsi slogan look and sound like informal American English by repeatedly omitting one letter:**

   Lipsmacking thirstquenching acetasting motivating goodbuzzing cooltalking highwalking fastliving evergiving coolfizzing Pepsi!

11 Bearing in mind that her accent drops h's and the endings of some words, have a go at breathing life into the character of this Cockney prostitute, simply with apostrophes. There are no absolutes here; just have a go, watching how your marks create her voice:

'Imagine though,' says Caroline. 'A picture of you still being there, hundreds of years after you've died. And if I pulled a face, that's the face I'd have forever … It makes me shiver, it does.'[12]

12 Correct these names and clarify the sentences using apostrophes:

 A   Scarlett OHara knew there were four is in Mississippi.

 B   Mr OMalley had lost all the as and us from his Scrabble set.

 C   Miss OReilly told me to change all my essay's His into Hellos.

A little trouble with names

That's us through the main roles of the apostrophe and it was fairly painless, wasn't it? Now, we step into treacherous waters, where personal judgement and – dare we say it – style come into play.

How, for example, do we indicate the possessive of a proper name, if that name ends in 's'? It is generally agreed that, with modern names, you should add an 's':

I read Dickens's *A Christmas Carol* in December every year.

Bridget Jones's Diary appeals to Chardonnay drinkers.

Alexis's shoulder pads were monumental.

However, personal choice is permissible if the additional possessive 's' might create some tongue-twisting:

Nicholas's / Nicholas' essays just weren't up to snuff.

Names ending in an 'iz' sound need no 's' to indicate possession. Nor does Jesus, if you mean the Man Himself.

Moses' tablets arrived well before Jesus' disciples turned up.

Similarly, classical or ancient names need only an apostrophe:

Socrates' philosophies shaped our ideas of ethics.

Mars' father was Juno.

However, when you take ancient names out of their context and use them elsewhere, they regain their need for an 's' to indicate possession:

The planet Mars's canals are sadly not what they appeared.

My dog Socrates's paws are filthy.

It's also worth bearing in mind that you should only use a possessive after the last item where two or more nouns are acting as one:

Even after all these years, I defy anyone to watch Torvill and Dean's 1984 Olympic performance of *Bolero* without getting goose bumps.

Things get less clear when companies, towns, tourist attractions, families and even events have stylistic or historic exceptions. This creates apparent anomalies like Lloyds TSB, Devils Tower, Hells Canyon, All Souls College, Bury St Edmunds and Guy Fawkes Day. These are all correct and just have to be remembered. It's best not to make assumptions, nor to get uptight (although you probably will, otherwise you wouldn't have bought this book).

A lesser role of the apostrophe is in the double possessive. Here (looking like a bit of punctuation overkill) both the possessive 'of' and the possessive apostrophe appear in the same sentence. This 'double whammy' is used to suggest something of a reciprocal relationship:

He was an avid fan of J D Salinger's. (He was a fan of JD Salinger, and, likewise, JD Salinger could number him as a fan.)

She inherited a letter of Queen Victoria's. (The letter belonged to Queen Victoria, and likewise, the Queen owned that letter.)

Note what happens without it:

She was a former girlfriend of the prince. (Doesn't that relationship look a little bit lop-sided?)

If you are not used to seeing the double possessive, you may be thrown for a minute into thinking you are looking at a badly punctuated plural, especially if there is no proper name involved:

He was a great admirer of the musician's. (One musician or many?)

She was an alleged confidante of the controversial journalist's. (One journalist or many?)

In such instances, the context will help you out – context being the unsung hero in the clarification of many, if not all, punctuation questions. If in doubt, look about; the resolution of every ambiguity lies in the words around it.

While not common, this 'double possessive' function of the apostrophe is sometimes particularly useful. See how the double possessive clarifies the following:

A photo of Audrey Hepburn's.

We can see that this is not a photo depicting Audrey Hepburn, but a photo the actress owned.

The double possessive doesn't work with inanimate things:

John Muir was a lifelong lover of Yosemite's.

That would have to have been one talented National Park.

That pretty much covers the roles of the apostrophe. Now it's time to take a closer look at some of these more problematic functions in action. See how you fare.

The apostrophe: exercise 2

1 **Complete the following:**

Chris _____ autobiography will have caused a few blushes.

A Evans   B Evans'   C Evans's

2 **Again, insert the appropriate possessive:**

Unsurpassed yet often variable; one way to describe _____ writings.

A Dickens   B Dickens's   C Dicken's

3 **Don't be put off by unusual last letters:**

I loved E. Annie _____ *The Shipping News*.

A Proulx'   B Proulx's   C Proulxs's

4 **Complete both of the following:**

Gabriel García _____ *One Hundred Years of Solitude* has been read from _____ End to John o' Groats.

A Márquez'   B Márquezs'   C Márquez's

A Lands   B Land's   C Lands'

5   This question is perhaps a little unfair, especially for non-UK readers. However, it is a very useful demonstration that, no matter how well-versed in punctuation you are, a good dictionary is still often needed. Contract the following as much as possible, while keeping an eye on misbehaving place names:

The Queen has never been to Queens College Cambridge, but did you say you are pretty sure she has been to Queens College Oxford?

6   Similar pitfalls can be found here. Place apostrophes where you see fit in the following:

A   I was supposed to be in St Albans, Vermont, for their All Saints Day service. It was just about Veterans Day before I damn well got there!

B   I've never liked April Fools Day; a practical jokes not everyones cup of tea, is it?

7   Which of the following is correct?

Jesus Cristiano Cervantes was an overweight plumber from Mexico City. Because he was an atheist _____ first name had always been an embarrassment.

A   Jesus   B   Jesus'   C   Jesus's

8   Complete these possessives as you see fit:

A   Of Jesus disciples, I think Thomas was probably the one I would most likely have drunk a beer with.

B   The goddess Venus beauty was fabled.

C   Of the Williams sisters, they say Venus serve is faster.

D   My cousin Martha's very well-travelled; next on her list are Harpers Ferry, West Virginia, and, for obvious reasons, Marthas Vineyard, New England.

The Apostrophe

9   **Complete these double possessives:**

    A Gaugin lived with Van Gogh for a few weeks. He was both a friend and rival of the artist, and similarly troubled.

    B When I tried to sell one of each, I found that a photo of Ernest Hemingway was less valuable than a photo of Hemingway that had been found at his Key West home.

    C It was a stonker, that speech of Churchill: 'We shall fight them on the beaches…'

    D It was no fault of yours and no fault of my mother either.

10   **Complete the following correctly:**

    A Those alibis of Burke and Hare — I just don't buy 'em!

    B It was a mutual friend of the couple who actually first introduced them.

11   **Choose from each of the following options:**

    A CS Lewis, fond of his ale, was a regular customer of The Eagle and Child/The Eagle and Child's.

    B Tolkien, too, was an enthusiastic supporter of the pub/pub's.

    C Mary Quant was an unparalleled icon of fashion/fashion's.

12   **Let the context help you out. One of the following should have a double possessive apostrophe:**

    A My boyfriend bought a lovely painting of Dali for a fiver in Camden market.

    B The most famous surrealist paintings of Dali now hang in the St Petersburg museum.

Catch My Meaning? Catch Your Breath:

The Comma

Nothing is more likely to cause a fist fight between two punctuation pedants than a comma. There are two reasons for this. The first is that there are fewer hard and fast rules to helpfully govern correctness for the comma than other punctuation marks; some areas of its use can be subjective. The second is that, historically, the comma has two ancient and distinct reasons for its existence. Growing old together like an ill-matched couple, these two forces are often at loggerheads.

Where did it come from?

The earliest punctuation dates back to 200 BC. At that time, it was used as a visual cue to help actors control their breathing during performance. For well over a thousand years, punctuation guided speakers (for that was what readers were) through the rhythm and accents of a text, rather than its grammar. However, from its beginnings in the 14th century, printing brought the written word and the once-exclusive skill of reading to Mr and Mrs Average. They no longer needed to listen to actors, storytellers and preachers to access writings; they could do so themselves. Gradually, the emphasis on performance was eroded to the point that we started to read into ourselves, rendering previous forms of punctuation irrelevant.

Enter Aldus Manutius the Elder (1450–1515), a Venetian printer who, with his son, took on the monumental task of creating a comprehensive system to illuminate meaning (and grammar), rather than melody. Their ground-breaking work provided the framework of what we know as punctuation today.

So what's this got to do with the comma? Well, think of the comma as the love-child of two mercurial and opposing parents: the written and the spoken word. Not only must it clarify the grammar of a sentence, but it still must, in Lynne Truss's words 'point up – rather in the manner of musical notation – such literary qualities as rhythm, direction, pitch, tone and flow'. That's a tall order for such a little guy. The unsuspecting punctuation mark arrived as a recognisable comma in 16th-century English and has been hard pressed ever since.

Warm-up

Let's just limber up to thinking about the comma and its power by playing a few punctuation games. Work quickly and don't get too hung up; go with your first instincts.

1   **Change the meaning of the following by adding, moving, or removing a comma:**

   A   It's raining cats and dogs.

   B   Let's draw, Auntie.

c   I'm tired of arguing kids.

d   When hunting, bears hide in the woods.

2   **Add commas as you see fit:**

A   A man may fight for many things: his country his principles his friends the glistening tear on the cheek of a golden child. But personally I'd mud-wrestle my own mother for a ton of cash an amusing clock and a stack of French porn.[1]

B   I could have eaten the whole packet of custard creams but I was on a diet.

c   I managed to eat only one; however I was still eyeing them greedily.

D   For God's sake do something!

E   It would be desirable if every government when it comes to power should have its old speeches burned.[2]

F   That would however be highly unlikely.

3   **Make this sentence less offensive to well-behaved rail enthusiasts:**

Trainspotters, who loiter on platforms late at night, are rarely to be trusted.

A tricksy little punctuation mark, I hear you cry. Well, yes, it can be. But it can do great things in the right hands. Let's learn how.

The comma: what should we use it for?

1   *To divide items in lists:*

A comma is used to divide each entry but is not habitually needed before the final 'and' (though we will qualify this rule for specific instances of the Oxford comma; see below). The comma is correct if it can be successfully replaced with either 'and' or 'or':

The ingredients for scones are simply flour, sugar, salt, butter, milk and an egg.

We had a busy time feeding the chickens, mucking out the byre, gathering eggs and repairing broken fences.

Mrs Miggins made it very clear that the options for dinner were hot pie, cold pie or starve.

That's all very logical (and law-abiding) so far. However, though a comma may not be needed before the final 'and', one is very often used. Meet the Oxford, or serial, comma:

He was a cad, a cheater, and a charmer.

My husband cleared the drains, the guttering, and the front path.

It's standard practice in the UK not to use this comma, though many do (notably Oxford University Press). The opposite applies in the States, though some remove it. Canada and Australia tend not to use it except to prevent ambiguity.

Whatever your feelings, it pays not to be inflexible. Some sentences are undeniably improved with an Oxford comma. Hear the weight of the final 'and' in both of the sentences above, reminding us again of the dual origins of the comma to mark both grammar and breath.

In a list of adjectives, use a comma where an 'and' would be appropriate:

The vestry clerk [...] is a short, pudgy little man ...[3]

'I'll tell it her,' said the Mock Turtle in a deep, hollow tone ...[4]

She was a thin, unkempt, sour young woman.

Don't use a comma when the adjectives work together as one describing unit. Here they are not layering on several additional qualities but are making one concerted effort:

He's a great little lad.

There was a terrified black cat cowering in the greenhouse.

The British red squirrel is one of our protected native species.

2 *When two sentences (two complete actions or thoughts) are joined together with conjunctions like 'for', 'and', 'nor', 'but', 'or', 'yet' and 'so':*

They drove overnight for Gretna Green, but they lost their nerve before Carlisle.

My sister is a musician of some distinction, yet I cannot play a note.

I had known him a long time, so I knew him better than most.

Two controversial things can happen with commas for joining. In the name of art, some writers drop the conjunction and insert a comma where a semicolon should be. This is the infamous comma splice; cause of much gnashing of teeth and rending of garments:

He appeared silently at her shoulder, she had always thought him slightly creepy.

Secondly, it's possibly even more wrong to use words like 'therefore', 'moreover', 'however' or 'nevertheless' instead of the usual joining words. They are not conjunctions and need firmer punctuation: more on those in the exercises later and in chapters to come; get that kettle on!

3   *To stand in for missing words:*

I ordered the Ploughman's; my husband, a balti.

Jane reads voraciously; her brother, not so much.

This use of the comma is increasingly rare.

4   *Use a comma before direct speech:*

The King looked anxiously at the White Rabbit, who said in a low voice, 'Your Majesty must cross-examine *this* witness.'[5]

This use of the comma is primarily to pause for breath and harks back to its use for guiding the voice. We now seem to prefer colons or no marks at all. At the end of the day the choice of whether to use it or not is yours, though you must be consistent at all costs. As Lynne Truss says, 'since this is a genuine old pause-for-breath use of the comma, however, it would be a shame to see it go.'

5   *To set off interjections:*

Bugger, I've lost my mobile phone!

Oh no, where did you lose it?

Hang on, I've found it, thank God.

6   *To encapsulate a portion of a sentence that's just bonus infor-mation. If you can take this 'weak interruption' out without losing the sentence meaning, close it off in commas:*

Writers, like teeth, are divided into incisors and grinders.[6]

Emma, who had not touched macaroni since university, couldn't bring herself to eat.

However, if by lifting out this portion you change the sentence's meaning, then you've got a 'defining clause' which shouldn't be put within commas. Quite the opposite is true; it must stay bedded into its sentence as part of its core meaning. Note the difference between the following:

I've noticed that Scots who love haggis are actually something of a rare breed.

I've noticed that Scots, who love haggis, are actually something of a rare breed.

The first sentence is correct; the second has a defining clause wrongly placed in commas. The resulting statement that Scots are a rare breed isn't quite true, is it?

When the weak interruption comes at the beginning or end of a sentence, only one comma is apparent:

Like teeth, writers are divided into incisors and grinders.
Writers are divided into incisors and grinders, like teeth.

These days, with a drive towards cleaner pages and fewer grammatical marks, you may find that commas for weak interruptions are omitted. Choosing to do so relies on context, style and personal preference, some of which we will touch on in the exercises to come. Is that kettle boiled yet?

More than any other punctuation mark, the comma's success relies on you being alert to the context and to potential confusion:

Clapham Police are searching for a burglar on the loose, wearing plus fours and wellies.

The Police are wearing what? Ronnie Barker was master of the comedic value of such ambiguities.

Does this whet your appetite? Enjoy the following exercises.

The comma: exercise 1

1   Punctuate the following lists as you see fit:

   A   We bought red wine crusty bread olives Stilton and Brie.

   B   Our hotel locations include Richelieu Azay-le-Rideau and Bourges to the east with Angers Champtoceaux and Pornic-Préfailles further west.

2   Each of these three lists could be construed in different ways. How could we instantly clarify what is intended?

   A   The pub's menu offered homemade soups, pints of prawns, beef and mushroom pies and toasties.

   B   We scoured everywhere for her: Harrods, Harvey Nicols, Hamleys and Fortnum and Mason.

3   Now try using commas to divide some lists of adjectives. Add commas where necessary:

   A   He greatly relished an American musical comedy.

   B   A single bright star shone in the sky.

   C   Psst! Want to know the secret to beautiful perfect-looking skin? Now it's at your fingertips with our detachable step-by-step guide.

   D   Each of their cars has an award-winning anti-lock braking system.

   E   She got through working life with a daily double espresso.

   F   She liked her coffee strong hot sweet and black.

G Not only did she need coffee; she also relied on her monthly financial statements.

4 **Use a joining comma and conjunction to make these two separate sentences into one:**

A They didn't have any mineral water. I got you a latte with extra cream and chocolate chips.

B I hadn't the heart to touch my breakfast. I told Jeeves to drink it himself.[7]

C They loathed each other. They married on a sunny afternoon in May.

5 **Which word or words are being implied by the comma here?**

A Thursday was bright and sunny; Friday, abysmal.

B For Christmas she received a diamond solitaire and undying love; he, socks.

6 **Omit some redundant words using the semicolon and comma construction as seen in rule 3 above. Used sparingly, you'll find it can provide a valuable change in rhythm:**

A Toby collected stamps and farming magazines. Stella collected unsavoury boyfriends.

B Mussolini had the eyes of a madman. Hitler had the moustache of a madman.

C Samuel possessed all the determination of a struggling but talented painter. Robin possessed the bank balance of one.

7 **Punctuate the following with commas only:**

A He struggled into the office wiped his brow and mumbled 'Boy Monday morning is a steep learning curve after a Sunday night out.'

B   The US novelist Raymond Chandler once said 'When I split an infinitive God damn it I split it so it stays split.'

C   To a woman heckler who cried 'You're drunk!' [Churchill] genially responded 'Ah but tomorrow I'll be sober and you'll still be ugly!'[8]

8   **Add a pair of commas to mark off the weak interruptions in each of the following. What is the resulting 'core' sentence?**

A   Liz Taylor as she didn't like to be called died in 2011.

B   Now thanks to celebrity baking shows key lime pie is making a comeback.

C   This morning as we waited in her dentist's waiting room she said she wasn't in the least bit nervous.

D   Every change in scene and there are many is marked by an overly long piece of dramatic music.

9   **What is wrong with each of the following? Correct them:**

A   The man, who is coming straight for us, looks very suspicious to me.

B   The remarkable Russian novelist, Leo Tolstoy, was father to 13 children.

C   Stephen Moffat's spellbinding storylines, for *Doctor Who*, have transformed family viewing.

D   Any man, that knows a bit of DIY, could tell you how to grout a bathroom.

10   **What two possible meanings could be taken from the following, dependent on punctuation?**

A   Teenagers who wear hoodies are a bit scary.

B   Chocolate cake which slices neatly is just no fun.

C   The badger which has endearing habits should be better protected.

11 **Where else in the sentences below could you put these interruptions, and how would you punctuate them?**

For example: He didn't, despite what I'd hoped, think much of Citizen Kane.

Despite what I'd hoped, he didn't think much of Citizen Kane.

A   Life, you know, is rather like opening a tin of sardines. We are all of us looking for the key.[9]

B   A vacuum can only exist, I imagine, by the things which enclose it.[10]

So we've learned about the comma and come out unscathed, so far. However, we must again dip a toe into icier waters where context, judgement, and the comma's opposing pulls between grammar and melody can complicate matters. Did you notice that Oxford comma there? I think I needed it, yet many of you will frown upon it. Yup, even I can't get through these 72 words without controversy; and so it begins.

The questionable comma

Well, we stumbled into the Oxford comma, so let's start this section by having a closer look at it. Some authorities, notably *Fowler's New Modern English Usage*, champion the Oxford comma, not only to avoid the ambiguities we saw in examples above, but in any instance where more than two words, phrases or groupings occur together in a sequence, e.g.:

Schoolchildren undertook a project on coastal, rural, and urban communities.

Ultimately, the choice is yours. The exercises later may help to determine whether you are for or against.

There is more to consider. Sometimes there is a clash between the comma's role to mark out grammar, and its usefulness to mark out breath:

> **Harry entered the ballroom, but failing to see her face in the crowd he turned to go.**

As Lynne Truss says, 'there are two proper uses of the comma in conflict here'. Some will see the comma being used as a joining comma before the conjunction 'but', where it provides a pause. Others will undoubtedly see it as the opening comma of a weak interruption that has, agonisingly, not been closed:

> **Harry entered the ballroom but, failing to see her face in the crowd, he turned to go.**

Sentences like this will always divide people. Perhaps it divides us into performers and grammarians; those who hear the sentence, and those who see it. Who knows? What *is* true is that our drive to make a choice between the two is recent. Read Charles Dickens's *A Christmas Tree* from 1850, for example. Phew! My English teacher would have drawn a skull and crossbones in my margin for punctuation like that.

And now we come to the question of the comma splice. Some argue that the comma splice can be acceptable[11], especially when the two sentences on either side of the splice are short, express contrast and suggest pace:

> **That's not writing, that's typing.[12]**

The world is disgracefully managed, one hardly knows to whom to complain.[13]

American editor, author, and language expert Barbara Wallraff observes that in a sentence such as 'It's not a comet, it's a meteor', using a semicolon 'would be like using a C-clamp to hold a sandwich together.' However, such learned advocates of an occasional comma splice recommend that if you are at all nervous of your ability to handle one acceptably, you shouldn't even try.

To get rid of a comma splice you have two choices: either join the sentences, or split them. Watch how both pace and meaning can change subtly. If you choose to use 'nevertheless', 'however', 'moreover', etc., remember they need heavier punctuation:

Splice: **I hope we don't have another bad winter, I am pretty sure we will.**

Fixes: **I hope we don't have another bad winter, yet I am pretty sure we will.**

I hope we don't have another bad winter; I am pretty sure we will.

I hope we don't have another bad winter. Nevertheless, I am pretty sure we will.

I hope we don't have another bad winter; however, I am pretty sure we will.

I hope we don't have another bad winter. I am pretty sure we will.

Now it's time to try some more tasks. The following exercises cannot test you on correctness, since much of what they explore is subjective. However, they will get you thinking about the more contentious uses of the comma and whether, indeed, you wish to enter that fray or steer well clear!

The comma: exercise 2

1   Where do you stand on the Oxford comma? There's only one way to find out. Punctuate the following in the way that you find comes most naturally:

   A   Revels come in orange raisin Malteser caramel chocolate and coffee. Coffee is by far my favourite.

   B   We stayed in Chattanooga Tupelo Memphis Mobile and lingered in New Orleans.

   C   They spent a sunny day collecting coloured stones seashells gull feathers and each other's sad stories.

   D   Churchill loved Krug champagne cigars painting and his country.

2   Here's an open question, just to put the cat amongst the pigeons. What do you think of this, probably the most famous comma splice of all? Is it acceptable or not?

   I came, I saw, I conquered.

   Would you change its punctuation? If so, to what would you change it? Do your actions change the suggestive meaning?

3   The following is an example of a comma splice, since its two complete thoughts are separated only by a comma. Apply all five options mentioned on the previous pages to fix it:

   I usually know what to say, I was dumbstruck.

4   Punctuate the following sentence from a TV listings magazine:

   Its lead actress Sofie Grabol is mesmerising as tough quiet watchful intelligent lead detective Sarah Lund ...[14]

A Theatrical Flourish:

The Colon and Semicolon

The Fred and Ginger of punctuation, the colon and semicolon have flair. They can make the difference between merely generating text, and creating art. They allow us to present words with subtlety, precision, and with suggestion beyond what we may be prepared to say. Yet they are enhancements; they are rarely necessary. Isn't it true, however, that it's the unnecessaries of life that make it worth living? So too with the colons, which make writing worth reading.

Some writers have spurned one or other of them; others have a worrying addiction. Ordinary punters, having heard tell that the colon and semicolon are old-fashioned, posh, or too difficult to tell apart, have discarded them for a scattering of dashes. Even Fleet Street recoils from them. But their mastery is well within reach. Why ignore such exquisite power?

Where did they come from?

The first semicolon was printed by Aldus Manutius the Elder in 1494. Similar marks had been variously used before that date in medieval manuscripts of psalms and Latin translations, and in Greek to indicate questions; but they bore little relation to what we in the English-speaking world use today. Though both the colon and semicolon had been adopted into English by the 17th century, they were tormented for more than a century by confused and changing rules. George Bernard Shaw, writing in 1924, was perhaps the first to offer a clear guide to their use. A word to the wise, however: do as he says; don't do as he do.

Warm-up

You may not have used colons or semicolons for a while, for fear of putting a foot wrong. You may use them abundantly, in a manner verging on obsessive-compulsive. Wherever you stand between those two poles, let's just warm up our synapses to thinking about these two versatile marks.

1   **Insert a colon or semicolon into the following gaps as you see fit:**

    A   There is only one thing wrong with this sentence__its punctuation.

    B   Let's do it__let's fall in love.

    C   I like work__it fascinates me. I can sit and look at it for hours. I love to keep it by me__the idea of getting rid of it nearly breaks my heart.[1]

    D   Turn up the lights__I don't want to go home in the dark.[2]

    E   You are a very poor soldier__a chocolate cream soldier![3]

2   **Punctuate the following using colons, semicolons and commas:**

Bo Peep had realised many things about herself she hated and had always hated sheep her dresses no matter how becoming were not the best attire for hauling ewes out of ditches men didn't like women who smelled of livestock and she was short-sighted.

3   Punctuate the following direct speech. Choose a colon, a semi-colon or a comma:

   A   'May I point out', she said__ 'that you have a rather large peacock in your living room?'

   B   With clenched teeth, suggestive of his temper, the General replied__ 'I am fully aware of its presence, madam. Are you aware that you have rather a dead fox about your neck?'

4   Correct the following incorrectly punctuated statement. There is more than one way:

   A   I am an eternal optimist, however, this is never going to work.

   B   There was only one solution, they would have to dig their way out.

Well, that may have been a tad alarming. Was it? If any of that unsettled you, don't worry; we're going to work through all the rules quite simply. Sparing you the other intestinal tract jokes, let's have a closer look at colons.

The colon: what should we use it for?

1   *To announce what is to come and invite the reader to find out:*

   Owen had finally faced the truth: he had no talent.

   Jane loved a lazy Sunday: old pubs, good beer, talk and open fires.

In Lynne Truss's words, 'colons introduce the part of a sentence that exemplifies, restates, elaborates, undermines, explains or balances the preceding part'. So, for example, the colons in the above sentences announce a logical conclusion to come. Notice, too, that a colon will nearly always be preceded by a complete sentence.

Colons also warn you that what follows may illuminate or undermine the first statement in a surprising way:

Being published by the Oxford University Press is rather like being married to a duchess: the honour is almost greater than the pleasure.[4]

I don't drink liquor: it makes me feel good.

Atticus was feeble: he was nearly fifty.[5]

2   *To act as a fulcrum between two dramatically opposed statements:*

In defeat unbeatable: in victory unbearable.[6]

She loved him entirely: he loathed her completely.

3   *To pull up the reader before something unexpected:*

She realised she felt something elusive, unsettling, and not unlike nausea: it was love!

4   *To introduce lists, especially those containing semicolons:*

Snow White knew her life was in a mess: no husband; no job; a wicked stepmother who, damn it, was much sexier than she was; annoying squirrels; and seven ugly flatmates who fancied her senseless.

But they are only used to precede a list if the sentence before it is complete:

A great holiday requires some raw materials: good company, a fistful of dollars, a few books and enough wine.

5   *To set off a book or film sub-title from the main title:*

2001: A Space Odyssey

Moondust: In Search of the Men Who Fell to Earth

6   *To separate dramatic characters from dialogue:*

Man: Is this the right room for an argument?

Other Man (*pause*): I've told you once.[7]

7   *They mark off direct speech of more than one sentence:*

I can imagine her talking to the sheriff: 'Well, sheriff, I hope your mother gets better soon. I had a cold and a bad sore throat last week myself. I've still got the sniffles. Tell her hello for me ...'[8]

If the piece of direct speech is short, it makes more sense to simply use a comma.

8   *Colons are also used to introduce examples:*

Just like this one.

That's it for the colon, then. What about its curvier counterpart?

The semicolon: what should we use it for?

1   *Most commonly, to divide two complete and related sentences where there is no conjunction, and where using a comma would be ungrammatical:*

Thank you for the manuscript; I shall lose no time in reading it.[9]

I think it's good for a writer to think he's dying; he works harder.[10]

The semicolon is, as we have seen, a stylistic choice, since a full stop is always a valid alternative. However, beyond the capabilities of the stolid full stop, the semicolon can provocatively link the very ideas it separates:

The hotel room felt empty; a small white envelope lay on my pillow.

Her fiancé loved the Eiffel Tower; she booked a honeymoon suite in Niagara Falls.

The tension created by the semicolon in each case opens up a suggestive world of inference, without stating anything conclusive. What a clever, and rather elegant, little mark.

2 *To strengthen division in a sentence or list that is already subdivided by commas:*

He ran straight for the metro, which was less than a mile away, and spotted her, alone, at the edge of the platform; but she didn't hear his calls, and boarded the train.

His sermon was a forthright denunciation of sin, an austere declaration of the motto on the wall behind him; he warned his flock against the evils of heady brews, gambling, and strange women.[11]

In a list whose items themselves contain commas, use a semicolon to distinguish how they are related:

We are delighted to welcome the Dean of the Graduate School, University of Tokyo; the Dean of Studies, Ecole Centrale, Paris; and the Vice Provost, University of Toronto.

Jo had an amazing three days in New York. Her credit card was hit hardest in Strand, the Broadway bookstore; Macy's, of course; Chocolate Haven, West Village; and, for her husband, Nintendo World, Rockefeller Plaza.

3 *To enable the use of link words such as 'however', 'also', 'nevertheless', 'consequently' and 'hence':*

Simon arrived, hopeful, and in good time; however, the lovely Miranda did not turn up.

He was heartbroken; nevertheless, he resolved not to waste a balmy evening or a new Armani shirt.

After the comma and its forays into the terrors of judgement and style, all of the above may seem comfortingly rule-based. Well, it's time to find out if it's really that easy. Get out your pen with an authoritative flourish. Who says this punctuation business ain't fun?

The colon and semicolon: exercise 1

1 Reconstruct these very logical sentences to include a colon. You will need to break them into two complementary halves. Remember that you may need to omit a word or two here and there:

A Richard was overjoyed. She had said yes.

B There was the key to his success; namely, the harder he worked the luckier he got.

C You have no other option but to try, try, try again.

D Rachel could not sing as she had lost her voice.

2 Add a colon to the following and allow the second sentence to il-luminate the meaning of the first in a surprising way. To maximise impact, you can often lose a few words from the second sentence, since a full sentence is not required after a colon:

A Running is best in the past tense. It is enjoyable only when it's done.

    B   She loved painting. But as it turned out, she was useless at it.

    C   I can do great things. I usually do them on a Wednesday, with fair seas and a following wind.

3   Just for fun, pare the following down to two dramatically opposed components, separated by a colon. Let the first sentence give you the lead to the shape of the second, and watch how the colon thrives on sparing text:

    A   She met him on a breezy Thursday morning. When he left her, it was a Monday night, and balmy.

    B   Preparedness is vital, so it is best to expect the unexpected.

4   Reconstruct these sentences to create a colon 'pull-up' effect:

    A   Laziness is the one trait in people that I can't stand.

    B   Rain is the abiding memory I have of all school trips.

    C   My face is spoiling this photo.

5   Which of these is correct?

    A   The recipe required butter, parmesan cheese, poppy seeds, sesame seeds and lollipop sticks.

    B   The recipe required: butter, parmesan cheese, poppy seeds, sesame seeds and lollipop sticks.

6   Which of these is correct?

    A   There are three kinds of lies: lies, damned lies, and statistics.

    B   There are three kinds of lies, lies, damned lies, and statistics.

7   Which of these lists is correctly punctuated?

    A   Marcie married Donald for: his gentleness; his fidelity, which had been tested and proven; his unswerving optimism; and for his passion, both for her, and for their life together.

B Marcie married Donald for many reasons: his gentleness; his fidelity, which had been tested and proven; his unswerving optimism; and for his passion, both for her, and for their life together.

8 Punctuate the following book and film titles and sub-titles using a colon. Even without knowing the titles, attention to the meaning will help place the colon:

A Never Eat Shredded Wheat The Geography We've Lost and How to Find it Again

B Parisian Chic A Style Guide

C Life and Laughing My Story

D Catherine of Aragon Henry's Spanish Queen

E Diary of a Wimpy Kid Rodrick Rules

9 Which of the following is correct?

A He cried out: 'Morning, gorgeous!'

B He said: 'My business is with the body. It's not my business to argue whether people are better alive or dead, or what happens to them after death. I only try to keep them alive.'[12]

C 'Well, well, well,' I said: 'who do you think you are, acting so high and mighty?'

D The defendant said that he was: 'at home watching CBS' when the crime took place.

10 Which of the following could, or indeed should, be linked with a semicolon?

A They are an odd couple. He is needy and she isn't.

B He is not really a novelist in this respect, he is a proselytiser.[13]

C   It's a world away from chasing aliens, as we saw Anderson in *The X Files*. Here she's a malevolent madam in Victorian London.

D   Summer is wonderful – warm days and long, light evenings.

E   I love spending time in libraries: any book I want just there for the taking.

F   He had but one eye, and the popular prejudice runs in favour of two.[14]

11 **What is being inferred by the semicolon use in each of the following?**

A   No news is good news; Jen heard fresh reports every 15 minutes.

B   She insisted on being buried under the apple tree; he chose a plot under the pear.

C   Their honeymoon was magical; he couldn't wait for it to end.

D   They divorced after ten great years; three weeks later Billy was a drunk.

12 **Strengthen the longest pause in the following with a semicolon. Also add commas where appropriate:**

A   Jem was the product of their first year of marriage four years later I was born and two years later our mother died from a sudden heart attack.[15]

B   Lastly she packed up her books quickly wrapping the most precious in clean white tissue paper for she couldn't bear to damage them.

13 **Punctuate the following correctly. There is more than one way to do so:**

A   I don't really understand the fascination with cricket, however I rather enjoy cucumber sandwiches and men in well-cut whites.

B   He'd bought her a fantastic pair of shoes, nevertheless he was still a two-timing pain in the ass.

C   She'd passed her final exams, moreover she'd managed it without losing her mind.

14   **Use a colon if appropriate, and semicolons if needed, to clarify the following lists:**

A   The evening will run to the following sequence, embarrassing name badge distribution, awkward mingling, a welcome address, a champagne reception, requiring inane sniggering at each other's anxious jokes, a colourless speech by V G Copperplate, Ministry of Indecipherable Signatures, followed by a five-course, silver-service, gala dinner and, thank God, carriages for midnight.

B   We will need quite a few things, pens, plain black biros preferably, paper, white, a dictionary for Neil, who can't spell, a thesaurus for Clare, who lost her adult vocabulary while on maternity leave, a large impressive desk, a whiteboard, markers, and, in case anyone gets hungry, a pizza menu.

C   For a really good Knickerbocker Glory you must have ice cream, in three flavours, if possible, fruit, cream, chopped nuts, chocolate sauce and a nice long spoon.

D   The trainer had done everything he could with the mare, he had broken her in slowly with the most up-to-date techniques, he had hired skilled, gentle stable-hands, all of whom had come with impressive references, he had sought the help of animal psychologists, flying them in from Vienna and Munich, and yet, despite all, the bloody horse would not run.

You see, it wasn't as complicated as you thought it might be, was it? That was all fairly well-behaved, and will set you up for pretty much everything you need to know about the colon and the semicolon. Refreshingly free of controversy, it's a shame these two marks are not used more confidently. There are just a couple of possible pitfalls to watch for. Read on to discover what they are.

Colon or semicolon? Dash it, who knows?

As we go along, you may be forgiven for thinking quietly to yourself that while this is all very lovely, it looks to me as if the colon and semicolon are interchangeable. Well, you won't be alone in thinking this, and in some cases they are. However, it might be worthwhile to just point up their differences a bit before we go further.

Take for example, the pairing of these two complete sentences:

She was panic-stricken. Her passport was gone.

Both a colon and semicolon could be used there, but, because the second sentence explains the reason *for* the first, a colon is far more appropriate. Listen out for a 'because' whispering stage left. If you hear one, it's a colon you need.

A colon is also more appropriate when you are moving from quite a general statement to a very specific one that illuminates the first:

Their whole house was reassuring: every room offered stillness, warmth and comfort.

Further, if the text after your proposed break is not a full sentence, remember you simply can't use a semicolon:

She had never noticed how unusual he was: a handsome sci-fi addict with good social skills.

With journalism wary of the colon and semicolon, a contemporary choice is to use a dash instead, particularly in place of the semicolon. Why? Well, the dash looks good, sounds conversational and, perhaps most crucially, you can't be accused of using it wrongly. However, it is worth noting that very different effects are achieved by the dash in comparison to the semicolon. Where the semicolon implies connection, the dash implies an aside, an afterthought, or disjunction:

> **I didn't bring my wallet; I left it in the car.** (*I left it for a very good reason.*)

> **I didn't bring my wallet – I left it in the car.** (*Oh hell, I am such a scatterbrain!*)

While this subtlety may be lost over time as we lean more heavily on the dash, isn't it heartening to be able to observe the distinction, and to use it while we still can?

On a more negative note, the semicolon's beguiling possibilities for suggestion can be tempting for lazy (or plain bad) writers. Pairing two tenuously linked sentences with a semicolon can be evocative in the right hands:

> **I watched my wife grasping nettles as she gardened; our marriage was a challenge.**

However, it can leave readers nonplussed in the wrong ones:

> **I watched my wife grasping nettles as she gardened; my career was a challenge.**

Eh? A writer might get away with it once, but after a while, he'll lose his readers: perhaps permanently.

The colon and semicolon: exercise 2

1   Add a semicolon or colon to the following as is most appropriate:

   A   They had never seen a painting like it. Murderous crows above a disturbingly animate cornfield.[16]

   B   He loved her. She was everything he wanted.

   C   The beach was beautiful. Above it, a single-track road rose into the valley.

   D   They wandered with no plans and without the pressures of time. Even their talk was languid and unhurried.

   E   As a child I loved riding. I like the smell of hot horses and old leather.

2   None of these three sentences is particularly striving to express the disjunction implied by the dash. So, how else could we correctly punctuate each of them?

   A   Chris's eyes sparkled. That's why Matt is such good casting – his eyes sparkle, too.

   B   The best thing about adulthood isn't owning a home or world travel – it's being able to buy your own snacks.

   C   As usual, Toby is feeling ostracised. Well, of course he is – he's a loser.

3   Have fun matching up the following with their conclusions. Note how some might create interesting effects in a couple of places; others will create nonsense best avoided:

   A   Lotte taught herself to play the guitar loudly;

   B   Louisa was teased as a child in Bari;

   C   Alice left the States for a new way of life;

The Colon and Semicolon

D   Samantha's biological clock was banging loudly in her ears;

E   Eleanor found a great job in the Embassy;

I   her red curls troubled her raven-haired classmates.

II   the couple next door were forgiving and tolerant.

III she was 38 with no boyfriend, never mind a husband.

IV she wasn't frightened of long hours or hard work.

V   Paris and its romance beckoned her.

Express Yourself:

The Expressive Marks

This is the chapter where an age-old maxim applies: less is more. We are about to step into the noisy, emotional and highly strung world of the expressive marks. The exclamation mark, the question mark, quotation marks, italics, dashes, brackets and the ellipsis are all profoundly personal. They help written text speak with a human voice to express its human qualities. As with all things powerful, overuse is counter-productive. The harder a voice strives to express itself, the less it seems to be heard; it's the punctuation equivalent of crying wolf. But handled with reserve, this family of marks brings life to words like no other.

Where did they come from?

The question mark first appeared way back in the 8th century and evolved, without fuss, into the question mark or 'query' as we know it today. The exclamation mark, its loud and slightly embarrassing counterpart, was first typeset in the 15th century and immediately attracted horrified gasps from grammarians if writers dared to overuse it. The same century brought us italic, a brilliant innovation that we've been merrily using and abusing ever since. The rounded brackets familiar to us today gained status later, when given an elegant name in the 16th century and writers inclined towards the feminine grace of the 'lunulae' over the angled variety. Quotation marks were still finding themselves in the 18th century however, with the jury still out even now on the question of double or single. Lastly, and despite what feels like a very modern vogue for the dash and the ellipsis in texting and email, it's worthwhile to remember not only that their names originate in Middle English and Ancient Greek, but that these marks were already great favourites of authors in the 19th century.

Warm-up

1   Add a question mark to the following where necessary:

   A   Juliet wondered whether her soufflé would turn out despite her having sunk a couple of gins while preparing it.

   B   Mike, noting her inebriation, asked if the dinner preparations were going okay.

2   Punctuate the following using italics and quotation marks as appropriate:

   The classic musical High Society includes unforgettable numbers like Well Did You Evah! and Who Wants to be a Millionaire? sung by a youthful Frank Sinatra.

3 **Are any italics needed in the following?**

They arrived en masse though there was little room in the house. Some set up tents in the garden and, despite inclement weather, doggedly ate breakfast, lunch and supper en plein air.

4 **Add quotation marks to this text:**

And I said to him, No Gavin, I will not take you back, no matter how many times you weep on the front doorstep till 4 a.m. singing Bryan Adams ballads. I never will. And when he heard that, he left for Amsterdam with that redhead from two doors down.

5 **Use brackets and change the word order to handle this information more concisely. You will need to change a word here or there. It's not necessarily a better way, just different:**

Jeff was feeling desperate about his weight gain. He hadn't seen his toes for a month.

Well that was an exhilarating dash through the more vocal representatives of punctuation. You may be feeling decidedly unfazed by our little test, or you may already be noticing that your understanding isn't quite as watertight as you had believed. Don't fret; it's time for all of us to knuckle down and become more skilful in this dark art.

The exclamation mark: what should we use it for?

1 *In involuntary ejaculations:*
   'Blimey! That's a big 'un!'
   'God damn! It got away!'

2   *To salute or invoke:*

'Bro! Great to see you!'

'O Romeo, Romeo! wherefore art thou Romeo?'[1]

3   *To exclaim (or admire):*

'Good Heaven!' said Scrooge, clasping his hands together, as he looked about him. 'I was bred in this place. I was a boy here!'[2]

'Why Grandma, what big, sharp teeth you've got!'

4   *For drama:*

They pushed open the door of the ruined mansion, each of them fallen strangely silent. Not one of them could ever have guessed what they would see, nor would have they believed that such a thing might be. But there, before them, lay a pale green dragon, sleeping peacefully upon a giant mound of gold! Treasure! And a mythical animal! Right here in Slough!

5   *To make a commonplace sentence more emphatic:*

'Digging for apples, indeed!' said the Rabbit angrily.[3]

'I could do with a little help here!'

The question mark: what should we use it for?

1   *To indicate a direct question:*

Who do you think you are?

How should I know?

2   *To indicate a question within quotation marks:*

'Haven't we met before?' he inquired, suggestively.

'Weren't you my Geography teacher?' she snarled.

When the question is indirect, no question mark is needed:

Where was he going with this, she wondered.

He poured her a dry martini, and asked if she'd like to hear about alluvial deposits.

Italics: what should we use them for?

1 *To indicate the titles of books, newspapers, magazines, albums, CDs, plays, films, TV and radio series, and many other complete works:*

Christopher Isherwood's life inspired the Hollywood films *Cabaret* and *A Single Man.*

She instantly regretted her centrefold photo shoot for *Penthouse.*

Not content with being brilliant in the US TV series *House,* Hugh Laurie has also released a blues album: *Let Them Talk.*

2 *To emphasise certain words:*

'I swear that's not *my* screaming toddler! Honestly; I have no idea *whose* child that is!'

Because of the law of diminishing returns, it's not a question of whether you *can* use italics for emphasis, but whether you *should.*

3 *To indicate foreign words and phrases:*

I've always thought the French phrase *le mot juste* says so much more than its limp English translation.

Italics are also used for foreign words which, though familiar, have not been fully assimilated into English:

Recruited into a Hitler Youth group at the age of 10, he joined the *Luftwaffe* as a radio operator at 16.

Chris loved chicken and he loved wine, so it seemed odd to his doting wife that he should so dislike her *coq au vin*.

If you have a good dictionary, you will find that those words which are classed as 'assimilated' will be in normal text, while those still seen as being foreign terms appear in italics. An example of a fully assimilated foreign term:

When her old geography teacher turned up again, she had a hideous sense of déjà vu.

4   *To indicate examples when writing about language itself:*

In the UK we spell *dolour* with a *u*, and get all hot under the collar when we see it without in American English. But we write *dolorous*, don't we?

The past tense of *forbid* has always given me trouble.

Quotation marks: what should we use them for?

Contemporary UK grammars enclose speech between single quotation marks and use double for a quotation within a quotation. However, the opposite order applies in the US, and indeed, in much UK journalism. I know; it's confusing. Well, actually, it's not really. As long as you decide on which rule works for you and stick to it, we can all get along fine. But don't mix and match; that's just not cricket. So, how do we use quotation marks again?

1   *To indicate direct speech:*

'Excuse me,' Cinderella blurted at the castle door, 'could you show me the way to Lost and Found?'

Quotation marks set off dialogue, with each speaker's words on a new line:

'What have you lost then, missy? I haven't got all day!'

'A glass slipper.'

'The shoes kids wear these days! You're better off with squirrel pelt – lets the feet breathe. Didn't your mother teach you anything?'

'Um, I don't have a mother.'

'Oh.'

2   *To indicate a quotation within a quotation:*

'There she was, standing at the door. And do you know what I says to her? I says, "Didn't your mother teach you anything?" And do you know what the poor mite says to me? She said, "I don't have a mother!" Oh, I did feel awful …'

At this point I should say that geography can have an effect on quotation marks, or the punctuation that surrounds them at least. UK style differs a little from that of the US and Canada, but we will go into that later and all will become clear.

3   *To highlight examples and words under discussion:*

I am bracing myself for another 'landmark' series on the history of the British Empire. Why is it that such programmes are always described as 'landmark'? Does anyone really know what 'landmark' actually means?

Much in the way that italics can pick out key words, quotation marks can do the same.

Dashes: what should we use them for?

1   *To connect or separate phrases or sentences:*

'Who is she? – Who can she be? – Whom did I ever hear him talk of as young and attractive among his female acquaintance? Oh! no one, no one – he talked to me only of myself.'[4]

In such examples the dash (normally an 'en rule', the same width as the average typeset character or the character 'n') denotes scattered thought, disjunction, hesitation, and says a lot about a character or their circumstances. A single dash (the word's root means *to break*) creates a break from what went before to get a reaction from you:

I'm not cheating anymore – and I did cheat.

I wasn't ashamed of what I had done. I was, well, what can one say – delighted!

I married beneath me – all women do.[5]

2   *To set off an interruption in a sentence that is stronger than can be achieved with commas or brackets:*

She gave up everything – absolutely everything – for her new life with him.

I've worked with several back-stabbing females before – 'bitches' if you like – but one will always stand out in my memory.

Used like this, the dash exclaims the bonus information rather than mumbling it discreetly, as brackets often do.

3   *To denote interruption both of direct speech and of a character's actions:*

'I haven't come all this way to fight, I—'

She moved carefully in the gloom, following the unexplained tapping coming from the cellar, when—

In this case most publishers use an em rule, as demonstrated in the examples above. Twice the length of the en rule, the em rule is also used by some publishing houses to perform the functions otherwise assigned to its shorter counterpart, but with the space closed on either side:

I'm not cheating anymore—and I did cheat.

It is particularly popular in North America and can also frequently be found in older texts – flick through some Dickens to see what I mean.

Brackets: what should we use them for?

In the US, brackets (like this) are called parentheses, while square brackets [like this] are simply called brackets. Sorted? Then we shall begin.

1   *To add information, to clarify, explain or illustrate:*

She wanted her children Samuel (4) and Bryony (2) to have the best of everything.

It was not to titillate that he wrote the (in)famous passages in *Lady Chatterley's Lover.*

Pete (who'd gazed at the stars since childhood) built himself a telescope from scratch.

2   *To slip in asides from the author:*

She's smart, gorgeous, talented and rich (do I sound bitter?).

On their reunion, the philandering singer claimed fidelity to his wife would become his driving passion (yeah, right!).

3 *Square brackets are used by an author or editor to clarify a direct quote without changing it:*

Perhaps that's why he [Jones] wears his erudition so lightly.

or

Perhaps that's why [Jones] wears his erudition so lightly.

Square brackets also enclose the word *sic*. This is a writer or editor saying the mistake here is not theirs:

Mr Ernest Pageworthy was a trusted employee of London's oldest pubic [sic] library.

Sometimes [sic] means that what precedes may look like a mistake but (sadly for some) it isn't:

At the age of 21, Norman Nomates [sic] legally changed his name.

4 *Occasionally, square brackets will enclose an ellipsis, where words are omitted:*

'She's half a witch, I think,' said Arthur Gride, when he found himself alone. 'But she's very frugal, and she's very deaf [...] She's a charming woman—for the purpose; a most discreet old housekeeper, and worth her weight in—copper.'[6]

The ellipsis: what should we use it for?

1 *To allow a sentence to trail off in a suggestive way:*

Physics has always been a closed book to me, but with a little effort I hope to see the light …

The timing isn't right in my life, but maybe in the next five years …

2 *To indicate that there are words missing from quoted material:*

The first part of their journey was performed in too melancholy a disposition to be otherwise than tedious and unpleasant. But … a view of Barton valley as they entered it gave them cheerfulness.[7]

Well, phew! That's that for the expressive marks. By now you should know what's coming. It's time to put you in the driving seat.

The expressive marks: exercise 1

1 Adapt the punctuation in the following texts to include as many exclamation marks as you think are required:

   A   'Wow,' cried Baby Bear, 'Mum, dad. There's a cute blonde in my bed.'

   B   'And a natural one at that,' exclaimed Mummy Bear, admiringly.

2 Add a question mark to the following in the correct place:

   A   Daddy Bear gasped, 'Son, what in God's name have you been up to.'

   B   Waking up into a full-blown domestic, Goldilocks wondered why on earth she'd thought breaking and entering was a good idea.

   C   'Why do you always have to jump to conclusions,' snapped Mummy Bear.

   D   Watching her leave, Baby Bear asked himself what might have happened if he'd got Goldilocks's mobile number.

3   **Underline any words which should be in italics and insert quotation marks where appropriate:**

   A   Aretha Franklin's masterpiece I Never Loved a Man the Way I Love You is the album in which the Queen of Soul finds her voice. Tracks include ageless hits like Respect, Dr Feelgood and Baby, Baby, Baby.

   B   An article on Macbeth called If Chance Would Have Me King was published in Fringe magazine last month; it attracted both critical acclaim and controversy.

   C   First screened in 1986, Beer was a particularly hilarious episode of the BBC TV series Blackadder, made even more memorable by Miriam Margolyes's aghast performance as Edmund's puritan aunt.

   D   Michelangelo's David is, undeniably, a fine figure of a man.

   E   Renoir's Girl with a Watering Can appeared in the Hollywood movies Possessed and Lady in the Lake, while Picasso's The Lovers can be spotted in the 1957 Hollywood musical, Funny Face.

   F   On April 17, 1975, Elvis bought a Convair 880 Jet and promptly named it the Lisa Marie.

   G   The Belle of Louisville is reputedly the oldest operating steamboat in the United States.

4   **Where might you use italics in the following?**

   A   They didn't have one, but three holidays a year.

   B   It's not the quantity that counts, but the quality.

   C   I can confidently state that your new boyfriend is not Elvis.

   D   It looks like a very handy gadget, but what does it do?

5   **Add italics to the following as you see fit:**

   A   After reading about the destructive tendencies of homo sapiens, Eva felt she'd lost her joie de vivre.

B   In the film Dead Poets Society, Robin Williams draws his students round a school photograph and exhorts them, sotto voce: 'Carpe diem. Seize the day, boys. Make your lives extraordinary.'

C   The lecturer droned on ad nauseum; Jamie committed the terrible faux pas of falling asleep in the front row during a televised lecture.

D   It was a fait accompli that Jamie's snooze would be caught on camera. Amongst the tutors of the University's ancien régime, he came to be seen as something of a bête noire.

E   'Well,' muttered Jamie en route home from his worst tutorial yet, 'c'est la vie.'

6   **Add italics (or quotation marks if you prefer) to the following where necessary:**

A   People seem to get terribly confused by there, their, and they're. I've never understood why.

B   Shouldn't we start a campaign to resurrect fabulous words that have fallen out of favour? On my list would be gems like ramshackle, ragamuffin, rapscallion and – the incomparable – swizz.

C   I still have to count out every s, every i, and every p in Mississippi, in the same way I have to say the letters of the alphabet out loud when I use a dictionary. It's slightly worrying.

D   When it comes to computing, what is the plural of mouse?

7   **Put the following into quotation marks (of your chosen number) and add the appropriate punctuation:**

A   I wonder, he murmured, touching her cheek, whether I might possibly come up for coffee

B   Excuse me mister, she spat, hands on ample hips, I ain't that kind of girl c   Do you know what he said to me, he said, Janice, I don't love you anymore, so I belted him, who the hell is Janice

8   **Where should the question mark be in the following?**

A   Why is it that, since 1977, I can only think of Luke Skywalker trying to blow up a Death Star when I hear the simple words 'almost there'

B   Was there ever a better understatement than 'Houston, we have a problem'

c   He seemed surprised when she gasped: 'I haven't seen you for a year and then you turn up out of the blue and ask me what's for dinner. Who the hell do you think you are'

9   **What are the alternative ways in which you could correctly punctuate the following?**

A   Simon Barnes asserts that nature, red in tooth and claw, is central to our well-being.

B   All sorts of characters, none of them appropriate, were in my head before I created the dark and intriguing detective.

c   Having apologised to their girlfriends, the boys, guilty and dejected, met for a taciturn pint.

D   The actress denied rumours that her lips, already a topic of hot internet debate, had been enlarged with collagen treatments.

10   **Use brackets to punctuate the following:**

A   Emma Harding who had never been inside an aeroplane until a month ago fulfilled her lifelong ambition today when she gained her pilot's licence.

B   Her children Luke 8 and Matilda 12 were present at her first admittedly erratic unaccompanied flight.

C Interviewed later, the children described how proud they were of their determined though sometimes unpredictable mother.

11 Slip in an aside, any aside, into the following, as long as you bracket it. Have fun; there will be no point scoring:

A He was young, stylish, and wealthy. Owner of an Aston Martin and 400 acres, and husband to a stunning blonde, he had every reason to be content in life.

B J. Lo has always claimed she's still Jenny from the block.

12 Add the necessary punctuation in and around these brackets:

A Their argument endured from dawn until dusk (For their tempestuous relationship, this was not unusual)

B Their argument endured from dawn until dusk (and was not unusual)

13 How would you deal with the following if you were the editor?

A In *On the Waterfront*, Marlon Brandow was unforgettable as Terry Malloy, brooding misfit of the New York Docks.

B Really Dull Street in Fresno was featured in a CBS news report about unbelievable place names.

14 Use ellipses to cut the word count of the following texts, without losing the core of what has been said:

A His ignorance was as remarkable as his knowledge. Of contemporary literature, philosophy and politics he appeared to know next to nothing. Upon my quoting Thomas Carlyle, he inquired in the naivest way who he might be and what he had done. My surprise reached a climax, however, when I found incidentally that he was ignorant of the Copernican Theory and of the composition of the Solar System. That any civilised human being in this nineteenth century should not be aware that the earth travelled round the sun appeared to be to me such an extraordinary fact that I could scarcely realise it.[8]

B   In April 2010 a woman was banned from entering Disneyland Paris because she was dressed as a princess. Despite having travelled from Coventry for the holiday of a lifetime, the crestfallen mum was forced to return to her hotel and change after she was told by staff that her costume might 'confuse' the children.

15   **Where might you use ellipsis to make these less informative and more suggestive?**

A   The question of whether computers will ever develop intuition throws up more interesting science and deep ideas than you might expect: the excellent Dr Hal Sinclair investigates in this award-winning documentary and decides, crushingly, that it definitely won't ever happen.

B   They'd shared a simple picnic in Central Park, sat close in a matinee movie, and held hands on the breezy top of the Empire State Building. Touching her hair as they waited in Grand Central Station, Tom asked haltingly if Marcy would like to come back to his place; Amazon had just delivered his remastered *Battlestar Galactica* box set and he'd gotten some microwave butter popcorn in specially. They could even push the boat out and order pizza if she was hungry, since his mom really didn't mind him having hot food in his room.

We have ways of making you talk

Now that we have run through all of the expressive marks, it may be time to pay just a bit of attention to one of the few problematic areas associated with these eloquent little symbols. Knowing how to position the punctuation in and around quotation marks can scare the living daylights out of some people. But as Douglas Adams said: DON'T PANIC.

When deciding how to punctuate around a quote, first think of the quote as if it were standing alone, let's say on a script for a play, where it would need a full stop to complete it:

Amy:	I bet you ten bucks you can't eat this doughnut without licking your lips.
Ben:	Oh, you think so, huh? Well, just watch me.
Amy:	I'm telling you, Shane; I feel richer already.
Ben:	See this sugar face? Pay up, lady!
Amy:	Double or quits! Let's go!

However, when turning this into a direct quote in a piece of text, we still need to attribute the speech to a speaker, so we can't close the spoken words with a full stop. Instead, a comma inside the quote marks 'represents' the full stop – it is closing that statement.

'I bet you ten bucks you can't eat this doughnut without licking your lips,' smirked Amy.

When speech is attributed at the start or in the middle, finish the whole thing with a full stop inside the quotation marks, as this final full stop will have to close the whole sentence off by itself:

'I bet you ten bucks', smirked Amy, 'you can't eat this doughnut without licking your lips.'

Ben coolly replied, 'Oh, you think so, huh? Well, just watch me.'

When the dialogue sits alone, the full stop also comes inside the quotation marks; again, this full stop will have to do all of the closing work unaided:

'I'm telling you, Ben; I feel richer already.'

When only a small snippet of speech is quoted, the punctuation sits outside the inverted commas, because the sentence will do the punctuation work, rather than the fragment:

Amy was always wary of his 'just watch me'; today was no exception.

There is a discrepancy between the US and UK usage at this particular point. Take a sentence that ends with a quoted phrase:

Amy knew to watch out for Ben's 'just watch me'. [*UK*]

In the UK we put the full stop outside the quotation marks, as we think it is the sentence which is delivering the meaning and doing the punctuation work. However, in the US and Canada, all the punctuation is gathered up inside the quotation mark, even though the quotation may itself be incomplete. To UK readers, it may seem counterintuitive, but it does look neat:

Amy knew to watch out for Ben's 'just watch me.' [*US*]

That's one of the few ways we differ: back to common ground.

When the quotation is a question or exclamation, the terminal marks come inside the quotation marks so that they can act on the spoken words inside. It doesn't matter where the speaker is attributed:

Victorious, Ben declared: 'See this sugar face? Pay up, lady!'

'Double or quits! Let's go!' cried Amy.

When the sentence asks a question, rather than the speaker or the spoken words, the question mark should go outside the quotation marks:

It had been his downfall countless times, so why couldn't Ben resist her goading to 'up the ante, fly boy'?

The expressive marks: exercise 2

1   **Punctuate the following appropriately:**

   A   'You will never have the balls to ask her out' said Robin.

   B   Nick set down his drink dejectedly and replied 'I'll prove you wrong. I just need the right moment'

   C   'Man, I don't mean to be funny, but you've been saying that for 18 months; you haven't got what it takes'

   D   Nick had always found 'I don't mean to be funny' to be a particularly ludicrous and offensive phrase.

2   **Which country do these punctuation styles correspond to? The UK or the US/Canada?**

   A   There was something forbidding in her voice when Miss Granger said he had to come to her office '9 a.m. sharp'.

   B   Billy knew he was in trouble when he overheard the words 'chill champagne' and 'expelling him.'

3   **Where should the full stop be here?**

   A   Never was a line more convincingly delivered by a child actor than Haley Joel Osment's 'I see dead people'

   B   After slaving in a grimy diner for three years to fund his thesis, Marvin folded his apron and swore, 'I will never touch mayonnaise again'

   C   Ed was nonplussed by her reaction to his well-meaning compliment that she was 'probably the second prettiest girl at the party'

When Words Collide:
The Hyphen

The hyphen is believed by some to be an endangered species. One of its key roles in creating compound words is particularly at risk. We are increasingly inclined towards 'closed' or 'open' compounds like 'backpack' and 'back burner' instead of their hyphenated counterparts. Tastes even differ here, with US English favouring the concise closed option, and UK English plumping for the (perhaps more staid) open alternatives. However, other dictionary-watchers believe that the hyphen, despite its removal from thousands of compounds over the past decade, has a long and active career ahead, albeit in reduced circumstances. What is undeniably true despite the debate is that no other punctuation mark is quite as buffeted by usage as the hyphen. Indeed, many weighty works on punctuation present rules for its use in a reactive way, stating that a form 'is now commonly employed and therefore acceptable', rather than the other way around. Though it may ultimately be for the boot, don't we owe the hyphen the courtesy of appreciating its many talents and using them to the best of our abilities? After all, it's our lack of confidence about using the mark correctly that has led to its diminishing job prospects. Let's not force an early retirement upon the hyphen – there's life in the old dog yet.

Where did it come from?

The word hyphen comes to us from Greek *huphen* meaning 'together', from *hupo* 'under' and hen 'one'. Hyphens have been found in manuscripts dating from the 14th century, with a comparable Hebrew symbol being used well before that. The first printed use of the hyphen is commonly attributed to Johannes Gutenberg of Mainz, Germany, in the second half of the 15th century. Creator of the Gutenberg press, the former goldsmith used a form of the hyphen to break words over line ends. The technique was perhaps most beautifully exemplified by the Gutenberg Bible, and echoed the hyphenation already present in the manuscripts from which the printer would have worked.

Warm-up

You know the formula by now: no preconceptions, no expectations; just rattle through the following questions going on gut instinct and what you already know of the hyphen. Any areas that draw a blank will be covered later in the rules, so fret not. Here we go, for the very last time.

1   Insert a hyphen into the following to clarify one possible meaning over another:

A She finally decided to end their long doomed relationship.

B Heartbroken, he took solace in ordering an extra large pizza.

2 **Hyphenate the following to express number:**

A He was pretty easy on the eye for a balding sixty two year old.

B It's said that only two thirds of Americans own a passport.

3 **What's wrong with this, apart from the fact you often get peckish at 10.15pm?**

Dinner is served from 18.00–22.00.

4 **What about these? Which areas of the following require hyphens?**

A The demands of his high maintenance wife were making him feel progressively run down.

B His hard pressed secretary couldn't fathom why her boss was suddenly so worn out too.

5 **Are these hyphens required?**

A Woodrow Wilson once said that the hyphen was the most un-American thing in the world.

B She had a post-Copernican vision of a Heliocentric Universe.

C This extremely valuable and obscenely ugly footstool is pre-1800.

6 **How do we sort out these colliding letters?**

A He had expertly deemphasised his part in the stag night fracas.

B She was now coowner of a new, sleek and rather enticing pink yacht.

7   **Would you add any hyphens to the following?**

   A   London was a melting pot; upper, middle and lower class citizens mingled in its unhygienic streets.

   B   She loved the design so much, she bought twelve first and six second class Christmas stamps.

Well, that was just a glimpse of what the hyphen is capable of. To learn more, and to answer the questions that you may already have, settle down and read on.

The hyphen: what should we use it for?

1   *To prevent ambiguity:*

   There is a world of a difference between:

   The Lone Ranger kicked at the long dead rattlesnake in his path, wondering whether his mother had repressed his best blue jeans or not.

   and

   The Lone Ranger kicked at the long-dead rattlesnake in his path, wondering whether his mother had re-pressed his best blue jeans or not.

The hyphen clarifies relationship; not only between words in a sentence, but between the component parts of a single word. In the first sentence the rattlesnake is long and dead. In the second it has been dead for a long time. Also in the second he ponders a laundering issue, while in the first ... well, it appears his mother may have somehow restrained his denims.

2   *To spell out numbers from 21 to 99:*

The Ultimate Answer to the Ultimate Question of Life, The Universe, and Everything is forty-two.

It was the twenty-second time he'd forgotten their wedding anniversary, and the first one-way plane ticket she'd ever bought.

3   *To create a connection between two unrelated words, or to specify range:*

In this specific function an 'en rule' appears with the space closed on either side, and works like 'to' or 'and':

The author–reader relationship.

The Hull–Zeebrugge ferry crossing.

Breakfast served 7.30–9.30 (never 'from 7.30–9.30'; use 'to' there instead)

Longer than a hyphen, this short dash demonstrates that you are pairing two previously distinct words, not hyphenating, for example, a proper name:

Lloyd-George, Britain's Prime Minister (1916–22), played a crucial role in the Paris Peace Conference of 1919.

It is a bit naughty to describe a role of the en rule here, when we are discussing the hyphen. However, it makes a lot of sense to group these meaningful little lines by their similar function, rather than looks.

4   *When a compound comes before a noun (or 'naming' word) to qualify it:*

The very same phrase will not need a hyphen if it comes *after* the noun:

We had four-o'clock cocktails, then a first-class meal.

It was probably the cocktails at four o'clock that made that meal taste so first class.

Londoners survived the Blitz in makeshift air-raid shelters.

The air raids were terrifying for everyone.

Christopher Marlowe was a 16th-century dramatist and a dark horse.

That dark horse Christopher Marlowe wrote his plays in the 16th century.

The hyphen is not needed where an adverb (usually a word ending in -*ly*) is used in a compound:

It was a hastily made decision.

She was a prettily dressed girl.

However, adverbs that do not end in -*ly*, like *much, well*, or *often* should be hyphenated before the noun:

Marilyn Monroe had a much-admired silhouette.

Marilyn Monroe's silhouette was much admired. You bet it was.

5   *In certain cases after a prefix, especially those before a capital, a proper name, a numeral, or a date:*

anti-Semitism

pseudo-Darwinian

post-Impressionism

pre-1900s

6   *To indicate that you want a word to be spelled out:*

She loathed it when people misspelled her name. 'No, no, it's D-A-H-L. Like the lentils!'

7   *To aid understanding and pronunciation when vowels or consonants collide:*

She came from Inverness-shire and was a pre-eminent scholar.

Still semi-illiterate aged eighteen, he went on to become a distinguished writer and broadcaster.

Hitch-hiking is becoming a thing of the past.

8   *To indicate that a word is unfinished and continues on the next line:*

    Pro-
nunciation
    Well-
    known

The hyphen resulting from the first example is a 'soft' or 'discretionary hyphen' while the second example demonstrates a 'hard hyphen', since it was keyed there already and provides the break. The rules that govern how we break words across a line end are determined by considering both pronunciation and the word's construction. To choose one over the other can yield unhelpful (if entertaining) results. You might, for example, want to take extra care with words like peerage, legend, and arsenic.

9   *To indicate hesitation or stammering:*

Mel: How long before we stop?
Terry: Eight hours!
Mel: D-D-Damn! I gotta go to the john![1]

'Uh-oh, I have a bad feeling about this …'

10 *To indicate a common second element in a list or a series:*

She had three uncontrollable children; a two-, a four- and a six-year-old.

Can you remember when we used to have first-, second- and third-class compartments on trains? With antimacassars? And smoking? Those were the days.

The hyphen: exercise 1

So, we've figured out what the hyphen is good at: it brings together words that are acting as one unit; it glues prefixes onto other words; and it holds other words (or bits of words) at arms' length from each other like a good boxing referee. Fundamentally, its job is to clarify both pronunciation and meaning. That all seems fairly straightforward; but is it? There is only one way to find out. Once more unto the breach, dear friends, once more.

1   Clarify the meaning of the following prefixes using a hyphen:

A   She redressed the catwalk volunteers under the watchful gaze of her terrifying boss.

B   The reformation has had global consequences. Everyone is coming to terms with the fact that Take That are getting on a bit.

C   After her favourite student was found cheating, Jess had to remark every paper.

D   Katie reserved the gateau after a couple of hours when they had room to eat it.

E   After protracted – but successful – contract negotiations, the infamous TV presenter finally resigned.

F   She had never recovered a cushion in that way before. But, by golly, there was a first time for everything.

2   **Hyphenate the following to aid understanding, prevent a change of sound, or simply for aesthetics:**

A   Harry made a preemptive strike for the first slice of chocolate gateau.

B   Emily was nervous about turning up on time for her preop.

C   The red squirrel has been largely ousted by the nonnative grey.

D   It is never easy to work parttime.

E   The honeymoon destination was nonnegotiable: Las Vegas or bust.

F   A word you hear less and less is *slaphappy*. If only it were true of the trait.

G   The letter on her doormat looked semiofficial and a bit threatening.

H   The second-rate thriller they had wasted good money on seeing was, well, thrillless.

I   One word of encouragement and she was reenergised for a week.

3   **Now clarify the following descriptive compounds with a hyphen:**

A   In the ballroom's Lost and Found, Dorothy found an exquisite pair of long forgotten dress gloves.

B   Arriving nervously at the Halloween party, Matt was faced by forty odd people drinking blood red punch.

C   As a trusted security guard at an exclusive New York hotel, he'd enjoyed a long standing career.

D   A renowned penny-pincher, Molly always kept a second hand towel in her bathroom.

E   Always prepared, her twin sister Milly always kept a second hand towel in her bathroom.

F   Graham eased himself comfortably into the first class seat he'd spotted that morning.

G   As a 40th birthday treat, she'd decided to buy herself an extra fast sports car.

H   Livid with his wayward wife, Mike began his cross questioning over the barbecue.

I   Two foot soldiers were found outrageously drunk while on duty.

4   Hyphenate the following if necessary:

A   Will you still need me, will you still feed me, when I'm sixty four?

B   Never one to miss good publicity, he gave away two thirds of his footballing salary on his twenty first birthday.

C   The fifty five year old broadcaster can still turn the heads of adoring twenty somethings.

D   The thirty year old British male is often motivated by the pursuit of curry.

5   Which of the following are correct?

A   The Dover–Calais ferry crossing fare starts at just £27.

B   Students should read and summarise pp. 90 – 132 for next Friday's tutorial.

C   Library opening hours are Monday–Saturday, 10.00–20.00.

D   Richard Burton and Elizabeth Taylor had a notoriously on–off relationship.

E   The First World War lasted from 1914–1918.

The Hyphen

6   **How many people are being talked about here?**

    A The Burns–Allen comedy formula took us from vaudeville to TV.

    B The Hyde-White performance style was reserved and wooden, but endearing.

    C The Fuller–Evers system of classification has redefined the way we identify some fish.

7   **Hyphenate the following where necessary:**

    A Her job was high profile, so she chose to date only high powered men.

    B Sara was completely disorganised; she hadn't had time to top up her phone or set up a new bank account.

    C Miles had stupidly hired a highly strung secretary with a waif like figure and a penchant for rice cakes.

    D Richard had made a well timed proposal. His rose tinted daydreams saw them as a happily married couple, while his realist streak fretted that Tamsin may require some extra marital thrills.

    E He came from a built up area rife with crime; nevertheless he'd built up quite a reputation as a nice guy who helped old ladies across the street.

    F Our newly designed anti ageing cream will reduce laugh line creasing and minimise even deep set wrinkles.

    G The film had an irresistible feel good factor.

8   **Which is correct?**

    A The Monica Lewinsky debacle effectively ended _____ feeling.

        I) pro-Clinton

        II) proClinton

        III) pro Clinton

B _____ is an example of an ancient parent language, or _____.

  I) Proto-Germanic

  II) ProtoGermanic

  III) protolanguage

  IV) proto-language

C Carl Sagan was probably the first scientist to explain _____ in an engaging way.

  I) anti-matter

  II) antimatter

D Maddie sprayed her cutlery – and husband – with _____ solution before every meal and constantly demanded _____ from her exasperated doctor.

  I) anti-bacterial

  II) antibacterial

  III) antibiotics

  IV) anti-biotics

E Face cream advertising relies on _____ terminology.

  I) quasiscientific

  II) quasi-scientific

F Our new neighbours were _____ ; thankfully they didn't try to convert us during dinner.

  I) Seventh Day Adventists

  II) Seventh-Day-Adventists

  III) Seventh-Day Adventists

9 How many hyphens should appear in the following sentences?

  A I write to you now, my fellow countrymen and women, in our hour of greatest need.

B I've seen some first, second and third rate movies in my time.

C He watched his shrewd investments gain in value; ten, a hundred, a thousandfold.

D He bought both the single and the double breasted suit.

E They were an Italian, French and English speaking family.

F The strike affected both blue and white collar workers.

To be or not to be?

Considering that the hyphen is thought by many to be on its way out, that's probably all the detail you will need to make your way merrily through life unencumbered by worry. However, if you are a glutton for punishment, or suffer night terrors caused by unanswered punctuation questions, then pray, step this way.

Many suffixes are so familiar that they do not require a hyphen. So, for example, we are used to seeing *nationwide, childlike, rainproof, clockwise and cityscape,* amongst others. However, if a combination is rare, is just emerging in English, or, indeed, if you have coined it yourself, then a hyphen is required:

He had exaggerated, almost conductor-like arm movements.

They conducted a house-wide search for Lemming, their escaped hamster.

Lily wore boyfriend-proof lipstick.

What do you think of this perfume smell-wise?

The cloud-scape at dawn was unforgettable.

So, how do you decide if a combination is newly coined or not? After all, it may be incredibly familiar to you. Well, the best advice is to check an up-to-date dictionary or, failing that, err on the side of caution. Sometimes a grey area is just that: grey.

Sometimes adjectives (that's 'describing' words to the uninitiated) are used with part of a verb (or 'doing' word) to make a super-descriptive combination like: *double-barrelled* or *light-footed*. When this happens, the compound must be hyphenated whether it comes before the noun or not:

> She had ensnared a good-looking man. Yes, he was good-looking all right.

> They bought a sofa on the day of their engagement. It was huge, and leather-upholstered.

Initially this may seem confusing since you've just learned earlier that only compounds *before* the noun should be hyphenated. However, it's like buying a new car; once you spot one adjective and verb compound, you see them everywhere. Once identified, you know exactly where to tuck that crucial little hyphen.

Now we move into controversial territory. As with a middle-aged woman whose hair is too long, sometimes the kindest thing you can do to a hyphen is cut it. It's all too easy to inflict hyphen fatigue:

> Our on-the-spot, face-to-face advice can be invaluable for first-time buyers.

> Money-saving tips for the recession-hit family.

Ugly, isn't it? Patterns like this appear a lot in advertising English, where information is crammed into the shortest word count or attention span possible. The trick for us laymen is not just to leave out the hyphens, but to avoid this trap in the first place by rewording with a tad more elegance.

The hyphen: exercise 2

1   **Is the following hyphenation necessary or not?**

A   Samuel was woken by an unsettling bell-like toll from the apartment above.

B   Since his Apollo missions, Alan Bean has painted moon-scapes almost obsessively.

C   Her manners were impeccable, her behaviour invariably lady-like.

D   The 2011 Royal Wedding was carefully orchestrated to boost morale UK-wide.

E   It was true. They stepped, spellbound, from the wardrobe into a magical snow-scape.

F   Industry-wide talks were hastily organised to prevent strike action.

G   Even by Ed's standards, turning up to babysit in a bullet-proof vest seemed a bit extreme.

H   It was parched and arid here. A desert-scape of ochre and red.

I   Sick of having peanuts pillaged, Bea resorted to a squirrel-proof feeder for her beloved finches.

J   He'd measured it length-wise, and completely miscalculated.

K   The splash-proof treatment Hannah had applied to her stunning suede boots was spectacularly ineffective.

L   Exasperated, she took over, other-wise he would have made the same mistake again.

M   Character-wise, I found the novel very disappointing.

2   Insert hyphens as necessary, paying close attention to the location
     and nature of the describing compounds:

   A   For the big screen adaptation he had to play a judge whose
        demeanour was constantly heavy hearted.

   B   The large scale production was often hindered by the
        tantrums of the director who was bad tempered.

   C   Thankfully the award winning producer was calm and clear
        sighted.

   D   It was a big break for the hard up lead actor: always quick
        witted and affable.

   E   As a peak time drama it should work; everyone loves a period
        piece set in the 19th century.

   F   Whatever happened, the final cut would be thought
        provoking.

3   Rephrase the following more elegantly:

   A   Late-nineteenth-century French art was dominated by
        Impressionism.

   B   Finally, older women can enjoy the confidence of age-spot-
        free skin.

   C   The ex-editor-in-chief was a grumpy man with a bulging
        waistline and an ego to match.

The Challenge

If you thought you were approaching a nice, fluffy, congratulatory denouement, then I am afraid you were wrong. Before that happens we must get our hands dirty – metaphorically at least. It's one thing to test your learning on clean-cut one-liners laid out neatly and numbered in an orderly fashion; it's quite another to get in and amongst sustained pieces of text with grey areas, non-standard punctuation and subjective stylistic choices. As with so many things in life, writing does not blithely follow rules, but bends, breaks, and sometimes arrogantly ignores them; mostly for artistic effect. As the punctuation maestro for the following passages, it's up to you, with knowledge and judgement in equal measure, to strike a path for both clarity and eloquence.

By now, you may be becoming aware that you have a very personal punctuation style. You may, for example, have discovered that you are comfortable with the Oxford comma (as I have done, in writing this book). You may find that you naturally avoid semicolons, favouring the decisiveness of the full stop between paired sentences instead. Whatever your preferences, one thing is true: punctuation is, when push comes to shove, subjective. Yes, large chunks of it are rule-based and therefore can categorically be described as right or wrong, but, in the same breath, a hefty chunk of punctuation is up for argument. It's the way in which you handle these choices that determine your own authorial (or editorial) voice. Bear this in mind when you check your answers at the back of the book. It is unlikely that what you will find there will exactly match your own responses. If and when they don't, pay attention to the divergence. Did you just slip, or is it an interesting variation that would stand up as valid? Note emerging patterns; they will eventually reveal your own – unique – punctuation signature. Be proud of it, for it is yours alone.

So how about it? Did you hear the unmistakeable slap of a gauntlet hitting the deck? Funny that; so did I.

1   **To get you warmed up and confident, here are some one-liners which, when punctuated incorrectly (as they all are), have an unfortunate double meaning. See if you can adapt the punctuation to reflect what the writer more likely wanted to say:**

   A   New boy band suffers hearing loss from girl's screaming.

   B   Owner of a successful events management company, Chris Cairns organises, parties, and functions, whatever your budget.

   C   Daisy's just in. Perfect for a summer wedding.

   D   It was ending the affair that destroyed his marriage.

   E   Free-range hen chicks please mind your step.

   F   For rent: secluded holiday cottage, perfect for couples with stunning views.

   G   Don't panic, breathe deeply, or swig a large brandy.

The Challenge

2 Here is a painful passage containing some of the habitual mistakes made by the average online reviewer. Resist the urge to put a line through the whole thing before rewriting it; all we need from you is to correct the glaring mistakes and add some clarifying punctuation:

In December 2009 I went to see Sorcery: The Legend in 3D, I was blown away as it immersed me into it's fictional world completely.

I received my copy of the Collectors edition earlier this week and have just watched it. This rereleased three disc version contains the original cut a previous rerelease version and seventeen minutes added footage. This footage does flesh out some of the characters and adds more of a back-ground including a brilliantly-added opening sequence with the much awaited high speed broom-stick chase.

Although the extra's are a bonus I am however disappointed. The film has been cut into two sections which means you have to change DVD's half-way through to continue viewing. Why could'nt the creator's, put the film on one DVD thus enhancing the viewing experience. What their thinking is behind this split elude's me completely, its very annoying.

The added material on this Collectors DVD is some compensation for the break half-way, I couldn't help but feel let down though, as a lot of the extra's mentioned on their advertisements are not included in the non Bluray version that I bought. Note to distributors people who don't have Bluray are'nt second class citizens.

If you're a fan of the film you will still enjoy the Collectors edition despite it's flaws.

3   In this passage you must watch particularly for semicolons, colons, commas and hyphens. Dashes will add appropriate volume to some pieces of bonus information. Beware of commas for weak interruptions. Some punctuation is wrong. Add quotation marks and their associated punctuation:

The wind howled. Aged sixteen away from home for his first lads holiday and secretly pining for the safety of his own bedroom Owen was terrified, he just couldn't let on that he was. Balanced precariously on an exposed remote hilltop overlooking the sea, their big decrepit and therefore cheap caravan shook every night. Of his five friends he found that the boys, who had been away before, were faring best. Admittedly however it was clear they were all miserable. The wind shrieked on. It was an unrelenting wind, an alarming wind, a wind that tore at their hair, it was a thief, a trickster, a mischievous imp snatching repeatedly at their over optimistic holiday clothes and driving sharp rain into their eyes. The boys avoided eye contact, all jokes were self consciously upbeat. Every last pretty girl had fled the beleaguered resort now, sandblasting was rough on their luminous complexions. God it was soul destroying, nevertheless he was determined to stick the holiday if you could call it that out. Those of the group, who had crueller natures, waited smugly for him to bail out, he would not. No way he muttered, Not in a million years.

4 **Focus on the sentence interruptions to gauge their relative volume and punctuate accordingly. Add hyphenation, apostrophes, italics, en rules, colons and semicolons:**

In the summer of 85 Susannah had been a smart beautiful girl with a bright future in the autumn of 94 she was a world weary housewife who today without a second's guilt had removed her cut price wedding ring for good.

Wearing a figure hugging dress that she'd bought only last week with money Greg had grudgingly given her to buy a new vacuum cleaner, Susannah snapped shut her faux leather suitcase, ran her eyes once round the ill fated bedroom and made for the door. Hollering brightly for Sam and Louisa, she scurried down the stairs like a flushed, hopeful teenager on a first date.

Downstairs, after buttoning up the kids coats, she stopped only to retrieve one further thing her copy of Its a Wonderful Life had long languished on Gregs tightly packed shelf of second rate horror movies.

In only twenty five minutes time she, Sam and Louisa would be on the Washington to New York to Boston line to join the friends and family she had mistakenly left behind to a new, well-furnished house they would call home to a secure job with great prospects to the care and support of friends, both hers and the children's to laughter, safety and happiness to a life without Greg O Keeffe. Perhaps Susannah might also find the one thing that had eluded her for nine wasted years love.

5   **In this piece, the stress of the boys' situation demands expressive punctuation. Their speech is informal, hurried, and disorganised. Listen out for each character's volume and punctuate accordingly. Watch out for hyphens, en rules, apostrophes and commas, and add quotation marks throughout.**

Hey. They are back. They are coming this way cried Rob.

Head in hands, Matt mumbled Good grief we are in trouble now.

She has brought reinforcements. There are three no four more of them wailed Harry. Who would have believed that a pretty though troublesome brunette would wreak such havoc for the sake of one ill-advised stag weekend kiss.

Quick. We have got to hide spluttered Rob.

Where in Gods name are we going to hide groaned Matt It is a beach for Petes sake.

Hang on surely not who is that with them stumbled Rob. Uh oh is it. No it couldn't but it looks just like is it. It can't be.

Yes it is. It is my future father in law gasped Harry. Well guys it has been a blast but I am out of here. As he scarpered barefoot and sunburned down the scalding white sand the boys could just hear him shout, See you at the wedding if there is one.

6 **You will need to think carefully about commas, colons, semicolons, italics, en rules and hyphens here:**

The foursome had put together a sumptuous picnic for their al fresco day of lazing in Hyde Park. After bickering in nearby delis they had acquired a feast par excellence two bottles of good red wine rye bread just baked three pungent cheeses olives potato salad hand cooked crisps crusted with sea salt four glossy pastries fresh cherries cashews dry roasted of course a large slab of very dark chocolate and one Gingham tablecloth. Natalie started with the olives Rose the cashews Ned and Marcus the red wine.

Now change any incorrect punctuation as well as adding in your own. Apostrophes and hyphens are important. Take care with italics again and allow the author to slip in an aside. A broken dream might best make itself heard from within paired dashes:

Before long conversation turned to what they believed to be lucid observations about life, it was always the same when wine was involved. Ned remarked that there was one thing that always disappointed him about picnics, lying on your stomach was never as comfortable as you expect. Marcus observed that there was a fairly effective solution to that, lying on your back. The girls opted out of the boys nonsensical sparrings, it was often the wisest course of action. Natalie stuck her attractive nose into Bill Brysons At Home A Short History of Private Life since having a home and an intimate normal private life instead of bumming about with a non committal boyfriend was something for which she dearly wished. The previous year had been her annus horribilis, Marcus had bought her a Wii Fit rather than a hoped for solitaire on her twenty ninth birthday. It was a painful insight into his priorities, and had taken some time to get over. In calculated retribution, she had forced him to spend Christmas at her parents house en famille. It was a satisfying if temporary revenge.

There is some incorrect punctuation here too. Consider commas, apostrophes, colons, hyphens, and italics. Watch out for Rose asking herself a question, and notice how one element of punctuation in particular can make her conscience seem all the more guilty:

Roses plans for the future were very different to Natalies, Ned didn't figure in them. She often wondered why the heck she had wasted so much time on him. Goodness the guy could be an idiot. Recently she had looked up a former boy-friend just for old times sake and found that after one clandestine caffè latte with him, she was reevaluating everything about her relationship with Ned. There was no doubt about it, Ned was for the boot.

7   **In this piece, allow the author to make a few muffled asides. Listen out for questions, add greater expression to the dialogue between characters and bring Rich's stammer to life. Watch for a comma splice and fix it. There are an opposing pair of sentences in there that need help too, while italics, apostrophes, dashes and hyphens could be important. There are deliberate mistakes:**

The newsroom of the Weekly Tribune and its hastily written supplements was a frenetic squalid and somewhat smelly place. Rich had until recently kept asking himself why he had ever wanted a job there. What had made it seem like such a good idea at the time. Perhaps Rich, accident prone, shy and blighted with a stammer from childhood, was trying to prove something to himself or as was far more likely to his unfeeling parents.

He shared a desk with a neurotic and under fed girl called Isobel. Isobel invariably looked as if she were badly in want of a meal, and seemed to survive joylessly on coffee, pre sliced fruit trays and Marlboro Lights. Surprisingly, given her job title of Features Editor, Isobel had a problem with even basic spelling and was continuously double checking with Rich rather than open a dictionary herself. His stammer often made such exchanges a little problematic.

'Rich! Recommend. Spell it for me?'

'RECCCOMMMEND.'

'Never. Goodness three of each?'

'No, I mmmean'

'Great Rich thanks, you're the best.'

Never having the time to wait for his hesitant explanations, Isobel would charge on recklessly, only to suffer the inevitable wrath of the Tribunes short tempered editor, Joe Jones JJ to both friends and enemies who fancied himself as the all powerful boss in Lou Grant. JJ even wore braces to underline the likeness which ended there and was doggedly working on attaining the fictional newsmans girth with a diet of glazed doughnuts, take out pizzas and full calorie Cokes. He was nauseating. Rich loathed him. Not only for his greasy faced smugness, but for the vindictive way in which he ridiculed his journalist's offerings, especially Isobels. For Rich was coming to realise one all important and assertive fact in his otherwise halting existence Isobel was the one.

8 Clarify pertinent information, meaning and correctness, while washing your hands of errors. Beware of hyphens and italics. Ensure that punctuation around quotes, and that which announces them, is correct:

Police arrested a man yesterday on suspicion of being repeatedly drunk and disorderly in charge of a horse. Arthur Brown 57 of Rossshire was spotted on several different occasions riding his seven year old grey mare Lusitania while apparently under the influence of alcohol. Local housewife and eyewitness Annie Keenan said You could see him riding down the High Street nearly every day barely staying on that poor animal. The beast just kept plodding towards home with Arthur swaying from side to side and hauling himself back up with the reins, singing at the top of his voice the whole time. His feet kept slipping out of them stirrups too and he'd have to shimmy about until he got them back in. Shocking it is although that lovely mare doesn't seem to mind at all.

Brown a local councillor stated that he had never touched a drop while riding and that his eccentric style of horsemanship was instead a new technique I have learned from Mortimer Drinkup. Mr Drinkup an ex horse whisperer who now organises combined riding and whisky tasting holidays in New England was unavailable for comment.

9 **You're on your own with this last one. Correct the incorrect, or add the missing, punctuation:**

Martha had discovered the joy of reading as a small child through some rather inappropriate texts. Her parents marriage counsellors as well as overworked doctors had a large white cupboard in their bedroom in which resided every book on marital discord ever written. These works contained details not only of the argumentative perils of finance division of duties and conflicting expectations but revelations of a more intimate kind ranging from couples with mis-matched pre and post nuptial appetites to some bewildering deviances which made Martha first wince then reread the relevant passages fascinatedly. After Martha volunteered a few startling terms from her impressive new vocabulary at a parish fund raiser declaring brightly that she'd learned them from Mummy and Daddys special books the cupboard was never left unlocked again.

So began her fascination with words albeit from an inauspicious start. A self sufficient and often remote child she graduated quickly from Danny the Champion of the World and Charlottes Web to darker tales that indulged her obsession with language. The Phantom Tolbooth peopled with marketeers selling pronouns by the pound was first to truly absorb her, followed swiftly by Alice in Wonderlands stumblings into the lifeblood of semantics. Ray Bradburys A Sound of Thunder in which one crushed butterfly changes the course of human and linguistic history was the short story she held responsible for her study of English Language at university.

In later life she'd heard tell of a website from which one could purchase words for charity. She blew three months wages on chiaroscuro, luminescence, quinquereme and opsimath before framing them expensively for her study. Having run out of cash she asked her husband sweetly if he'd buy serenity for her forty second birthday. He agreed throwing in devotion for good luck.

The Last Crusade

This is the end of our journey together. By now, you are an accomplished ambassador for punctuation, ready to strike a path for clarity and eloquence in a hostile world. Both you and I would do well to remember, however, that ours is not a static skill, but one that must reflect inevitable change, prevailing tastes and the effects of outside influences. Language, and its punctuation, cannot live in an ivory tower. It must immerse itself in the mêlée of living and the talk that living generates, so we will ever remain apprentices. There will be grey areas to deal with of ever-increasing variety, but with knowledge and judgement in equal measure we can stay both correct and responsive.

Before you go, indulge yourself and me with one last test of your mettle. The following is a tongue-in-cheek sprint through everything we have learned on our travels. Enjoy!

1   **A Christian bookshop has an advertisement in its window:**

Jesus's new writings: half-price sale!

   A   Did you miss the second coming entirely?

B It isn't Him. As the little boy says in *Whistle Down the Wind*, 'It's not Jesus, it's just a fella.'

2   **She's always said she was a lover of St Alban's.**

A By gum, she must be getting on a bit, and are saints allowed to behave like that?

B If she likes it that much, you would think she would know how to spell it, and not to expect too much in the way of romance from a town.

3   **That's no moon, it's a space station.**

A Isn't that a line from Alec Guinness as Obi Wan Kenobi in Star Wars? I wonder whether there was a comma splice in the script?

B Even if there was, it would be acceptable.

4   **What's wrong with this statement?**

The White House's most famous intern, Monica Lewinsky, was photographed shopping in New York yesterday.

A Her name shouldn't be in commas as it's a defining clause.

B Actually nothing. There is only one intern that famous.

5   **On Sunday we visited: Buckingham Palace, Madame Tussauds, Tate Modern, the Victoria and Albert and the London Eye.**

A A well-placed Oxford comma wouldn't go amiss in there. Tussauds is fine. I am sure they dropped the apostrophe.

B Yes, quite; but what's with the colon?

6   **I love you. Do you hear?**

A I never knew you felt so strongly!

B Oh, do you? That's nice. Actually I do have good hearing, thanks. Regarding the former – a nice little semicolon and I might have believed you …

7 Police apprehended a youth driving over the speed limit who swore he had 'only had one beer.' On which side of the road was he probably driving?

A It's anyone's guess.

B I'll put my money on the right hand side.

8 Muffle Marion's secret by punctuating this sentence fully: 'Marion who despised blind dates arrived for her third one that week.'

A Commas, brackets or dashes will do.

B Only brackets will effectively muffle the volume of what she thinks about blind dates.

9 What's wrong with the following?

He was a hair-brained inventor; always mean spirited too.

A Nothing; it's spot on. Hyphenate before the noun, not after.

B The compound after the noun should actually be hyphenated: it's an adjective + verb compound.

10 Hyphenate the following properly:

Welcome to our award winning, all inclusive, family owned, holiday complex.

A Welcome to our award-winning, all-inclusive, family-owned holiday complex.

B No, thanks. I'll rewrite it.

The results

If you answered mostly A:
You have a firm grasp on punctuation and have learned much on our little tour. You can sleep easy at night, knowing that your command of punctuation is thorough and admirable. People in your office will now pester you daily asking for advice, and it is likely you will become known as something of an authority. One thing: don't be complacent. There is always more to know.

If you answered mostly B:
You have a bit of a flair for this punctuation malarkey, don't you? It's likely you are known as something of a pedant/a little bit odd, but the chances are you probably like it. You have attained an enviable mastery of punctuation. Perhaps this book was, for you, merely a pleasant diversion on a wet Wednesday afternoon. Whatever is true, I take my hat off to you. Now get out there and spread the word; tell your mates to mind their semicolons. Our work here is done, but yours never will be.

Answers

At Your Service, Master: The Apostrophe

Warm-up

1 **A** She didn't believe that he'd ever return to their house's fireside.

   B He hadn't shown up since 1987. But if her mother said he'd turn up in two weeks' time, she'd probably be right.

2 **A** Come on Dover, move yer bloomin' arse!

   B In 'ertford, 'ereford and 'ampshire, 'urricanes 'ardly ever 'appen.

Exercise 1

1 There is an iron 'scold's bridle' in Walton Church. They used these things in ancient days for curbing women's tongues. They have given up the attempt now. I suppose iron was getting scarce, and nothing else would be strong enough.

2 **A** It currently refers to the toys for one boy. They meant to say Boys' toys.

   B It currently refers to the toys for one girl. They meant to say Girls' toys.

   C It currently refers to the toys for one kid. They meant to say Kids' DVDs.

3 It currently says 'no one dog is allowed'. (That is, a contraction rather than a plural.) They presumably meant to say 'No dogs allowed, please'.

4 **A** More than one newspaper has been ruined by the brilliant writer in the editor's chair.

   B A beginner's guide to catching up online.

   C The lads' big night out went tits up. Their two minibuses' exhausts were plugged by a hen party gone bad.

   D Their horror stories' similarities were remarkable.

5 **A** 'There she goes,' he said, 'there she goes, with two pounds' worth of food on board that belongs to me, and that I haven't had.'

   B In two weeks' time I'll be drinking cold cider in Somerset, but I'm giving my boss not one sodding day's notice.

6 **A** A woman's work is never done.

   B Let's have a drink for old times' sake. ('Times' are plural here, hence the placement of the apostrophe.)

   C Hurry up, for Pete's sake!

7 **A** The last moon landing was in the winter of '72, the year I was born.

   B My mum wore miniskirts in the '60s; did yours?

   C I was in the class of '92. It was a big 'un.

The apostrophe is especially valuable in the last example; here it acts both to contract the date and to clarify the class size.

8 'It's' and 'its' are simple really; the confusion has only come about because everyone else keeps getting it wrong.

   A It's not over 'til the fat lady sings.

   B The dog has had its day.

   C It's a Wonderful Life.

Answers – The Apostrophe

D   Any colour – so long as it's black.

E   The yard was so dark that even Scrooge, who knew its every stone, was fain to grope with his hands.

9   Would've, could've, should've. The bottom line is we didn't do it.

10 Lipsmackin' thirstquenchin' acetastin' motivatin' goodbuzzin' cooltalkin' highwalkin' fastlivin' evergivin' coolfizzin' Pepsi!

11 Author Michael Faber used the following apostrophes to indicate his character's Cockney accent:

'Imagine though,' says Caroline. 'A picture of you still bein' there, 'undreds of years after you've died. An' if I pulled a face, that's the face I'd 'ave forever… It makes me shiver, it does.'

12 A   Scarlett O'Hara knew there were four i's in Mississippi.

B   Mr O'Malley had lost all the a's and u's from his Scrabble set.

C   Miss O'Reilly told me to change all my essay's Hi's into Hello's.

Exercise 2

1   C: Chris Evans's autobiography will have caused a few blushes.

2   B: Unsurpassed yet often variable; one way to describe Dickens's writings.

3   B: I loved E. Annie Proulx's *The Shipping News*.

4   C and B: Gabriel García Márquez's *One Hundred Years of Solitude* has been read from Land's End to John o' Groats.

5   The Queen's never been to Queens' College Cambridge, but did you say you're pretty sure she's been to Queen's College Oxford?

6 A I was supposed to be in St Albans, Vermont, for their All Saints' Day service. It was just about Veterans Day before I damn well got there!

  B I've never liked April Fools' Day; a practical joke's not everyone's cup of tea, is it?

7 A: Jesus Cristiano Cervantes was an overweight plumber from Mexico City. Because he was an atheist, Jesus's first name had always been an embarrassment.

8 A Of Jesus' disciples, I think Thomas was probably the one I would most likely have drunk a beer with.

  B The goddess Venus' beauty was fabled.

  C Of the Williams sisters, they say Venus's serve is faster.

  D My cousin Martha's very well-travelled; next on her list are Harpers Ferry, West Virginia and, for obvious reasons, Martha's Vineyard, New England.

9 A Gaugin lived with Van Gogh for a few weeks. He was both a friend and rival of the artist's, and similarly troubled.

  B When I tried to sell one of each, I found that a photo of Ernest Hemingway was less valuable than a photo of Hemingway's that had been found at his Key West home.

  C It was a stonker, that speech of Churchill's: 'We shall fight them on the beaches...'

  D It was no fault of yours and no fault of my mother's either.

10 A Those alibis of Burke and Hare's – I just don't buy 'em!

  B It was a mutual friend of the couple's who actually first introduced them.

11 A CS Lewis, fond of his ale, was a regular customer of The Eagle and Child.

B Tolkien, too, was an enthusiastic supporter of the pub.

C Mary Quant was an unparalleled icon of fashion.

12 A My boyfriend bought a lovely painting of Dali for a fiver in Camden market.

B The most famous surrealist paintings of Dali's now hang in the St Petersburg museum.

Catch My Meaning? Catch Your Breath: The Comma

Warm-up

1 A It's raining, cats and dogs. (The owner draws her pets' attention to the weather.)

B Let's draw Auntie.

C I'm tired of arguing, kids. (The kind of thing an exasperated mum shouts from the cooker while her teenage children rail against tidying their smelly, hormonal bedrooms.)

D When hunting bears, hide in the woods.

2 A A man may fight for many things: his country, his principles, his friends, the glistening tear on the cheek of a golden child. But personally I'd mud-wrestle my own mother for a ton of cash, an amusing clock and a stack of French porn.

B I could have eaten the whole packet of custard creams, but I was on a diet.

C I managed to eat only one; however, I was still eyeing them greedily.

D For God's sake, do something!

    E   It would be desirable if every government, when it comes to power, should have its old speeches burned.

    F   That would, however, be highly unlikely.

3   Trainspotters who loiter on platforms late at night are rarely to be trusted.

Exercise 1

1   We have not used the Oxford comma but you could if you wanted to:

    A   We bought red wine, crusty bread, olives, Stilton and Brie.

    B   Our hotel locations include Richelieu, Azay-le-Rideau and Bourges to the east, with Angers, Champtoceaux and Pornic-Préfailles further west.

2   We could clarify each of them by adding an Oxford Comma:

    A   The pub's menu offered homemade soups, pints of prawns, beef and mushroom pies, and toasties.

    B   We scoured everywhere for her; Harrods, Harvey Nicols, Hamleys, and Fortnum and Mason.

3   A   He greatly relished an American musical comedy.

    B   A single bright star shone in the sky.

    C   Psst! Want to know the secret to beautiful, perfect-looking skin? Now it's at your fingertips with our detachable step-by-step guide.

    D   Each of their cars has an award-winning anti-lock braking system.

    E   She got through working life with a daily double espresso.

    F   She liked her coffee strong, hot, sweet and black. (Some of you may be itching to add an Oxford comma there, to add force to the coffee's blackness!)

G   Not only did she need coffee; she relied on her monthly financial statements.

4   Anything along the lines of the following will do:

   A   They didn't have any mineral water, but I got you a latte with extra cream and chocolate chips.

   B   I hadn't the heart to touch my breakfast, so I told Jeeves to drink it himself.

   C   They loathed each other, yet they married on a sunny afternoon in May.

5   A   Thursday was bright and sunny; Friday (was) abysmal.

   B   For Christmas she received a diamond solitaire and undying love; he (received) socks.

6   A   Toby collected stamps and farming magazines; Stella, unsavoury boyfriends.

   B   Mussolini had the eyes of a madman; Hitler, the moustache.

   C   Samuel possessed all the determination of a struggling but talented painter; Robin, the bank balance.

7   A   He struggled into the office, wiped his brow and mumbled, 'Boy, Monday morning is a steep learning curve after a Sunday night out.'

   B   The US novelist Raymond Chandler once said, 'When I split an infinitive, God damn it, I split it so it stays split.'

   C   To a woman heckler who cried, 'You're drunk!', [Churchill] genially responded, 'Ah, but tomorrow I'll be sober, and you'll still be ugly!'

8   A   Liz Taylor, as she didn't like to be called, died in 2011. *Liz Taylor died in 2011.*

B Now, thanks to celebrity baking shows, key lime pie is making a comeback. *Now key lime pie is making a comeback.*

C This morning, as we waited in her dentist's waiting room, she said she wasn't in the least bit nervous. *This morning she said she wasn't in the least bit nervous.*

D Every change in scene, and there are many, is marked by an overly long piece of dramatic music. *Every change in scene is marked by an overlong piece of dramatic music.*

9   In each of the following a defining clause has been put in commas, making it appear like a weak interruption. However, the information being held off in the commas actually defines the meaning of the whole sentence so should not be in commas:

A The man who is coming straight for us looks very suspicious to me.

B The remarkable Russian novelist Leo Tolstoy was father to 13 children.

C Stephen Moffat's spellbinding storylines for *Doctor Who* have transformed family viewing.

D Any man that knows a bit of DIY could tell you how to grout a bathroom.

10 **A** If you add a pair of commas, you are stating that all teenagers are scary, and, incidentally, that they all wear hoodies too. If you leave the sentence without commas then you are asserting that only hoodie-wearing teenagers are scary.

B By adding a pair of commas, you are asserting that all chocolate cakes are dull, and, incidentally, that they all slice neatly too. How annoying. Without commas, it simply means that you find easily sliceable chocolate cakes no fun, just like the lovely Nigella.

c Left as is (without commas), this statement asserts that only one badger, distinguished from his peers by his particularly endearing habits, deserves to be protected. If you add a pair of commas to mark off the weak interruption, you are instead asserting that the badger species (or simply all badgers) should be better protected.

11 A You know, life is rather like opening a tin of sardines. We are all of us looking for the key. / Life is rather like opening a tin of sardines, you know. We are all of us looking for the key.

B A vacuum can only exist by the things which enclose it, I imagine.

Exercise 2

1 A Revels come in orange, raisin, Malteser, caramel, chocolate and coffee. Coffee is by far my favourite.

B We stayed in Chattanooga, Tupelo, Memphis, Mobile and lingered in New Orleans.

C They spent a sunny day collecting coloured stones, seashells, gull feathers and each other's sad stories.

D Churchill loved Krug champagne, cigars, painting and his country.

None of these sentences *requires* an Oxford comma, though you may find that adding one can create desirable effect.

2 You may have decided to re-punctuate this well-known saying in either of these two ways:

I came; I saw; I conquered.

I came. I saw. I conquered.

Where the original's light and pacey punctuation suggests that conquest was an easy and logical conclusion, heavier punctuation implies a harder conquest. In fact, each semicolon feels like a tussle; each full stop more like a battle. Heavier punctuation makes the conquest a progressively hard-fought victory.

3   I usually know what to say, *but* I was dumbstruck.

I usually know what to say; I was dumbstruck.

I usually know what to say. *Nevertheless,/However,* I was dumbstruck.

I usually know what to say; *nevertheless,/however,* I was dumbstruck.

I usually know what to say. I was dumbstruck.

4   The actual punctuation in print was as follows:

Its lead actress, Sofie Grabol, is mesmerising as tough, quiet, watchful, intelligent lead detective Sarah Lund ...

Unusually here, the actress's name is a true 'weak interruption'. The 'its' refers to a specific programme, and 'lead actress' points to one specific female in the cast. Her name is effectively redundant.

A Theatrical Flourish: The Colon and Semicolon

Warm-up

1   A   There is only one thing wrong with this sentence: its punctuation.

B   Let's do it; let's fall in love. / Let's do it: let's fall in love.

C   I like work; it fascinates me. I can sit and look at it for hours. I love to keep it by me; the idea of getting rid of it nearly breaks my heart.

D   Turn up the lights; I don't want to go home in the dark.

E   You are a very poor soldier: a chocolate cream soldier!

2   Bo Peep had realised many things about herself: she hated, and had always hated, sheep; her dresses, no matter how becoming, were not the best attire for hauling ewes out of ditches; men didn't like women who smelled of livestock; and she was short-sighted.

3   A   'May I point out', she said, 'that you have a rather large peacock in your living room?'

     B   With clenched teeth, suggestive of his temper, the General replied: 'I am fully aware of its presence, madam. Are you aware that you have rather a dead fox about your neck?'

4   A   I am an eternal optimist. However, this is never going to work. / I am an eternal optimist; however, this is never going to work.

     B   There was only one solution. They would have to dig their way out. / There was only one solution: they would have to dig their way out. / There was only one solution; they would have to dig their way out.

Exercise 1

1   A   Richard was overjoyed: she had said yes.

     B   There was the key to his success: the harder he worked the luckier he got.

     C   You have no other option: try, try, try again.

     D   Rachel could not sing: she had lost her voice.

Each of the examples above can switch order over the colon with little, if any, change in meaning. *For example:* She had said yes: Richard was overjoyed.

2   A   Running is best in the past tense: enjoyable only when it's done.

     B   She loved painting: she was useless at it.

   c   I can do great things: usually on a Wednesday, with fair seas and a following wind.

3   A   She met him on a breezy Thursday morning: he left her on a balmy Monday night.

   B   Preparedness is vital: expect the unexpected.

4   A   There is one trait that I can't stand in people: laziness.

   B   I have an/one abiding memory of school trips: rain.

   c   There is something/one thing spoiling this photo: my face.

5   A: The recipe required butter, parmesan cheese, poppy seeds, sesame seeds and lollipop sticks.

A colon can only be used before a list if the information before it can stand on its own. To warrant the use of a colon, the example above would have to become, for example:

The recipe required only a few items: butter, parmesan cheese, poppy seeds, sesame seeds and lollipop sticks.

6   A: There are three kinds of lies: lies, damned lies, and statistics.

7   A: Marcie married Donald for many reasons: his gentleness; his fidelity, which had been tested and proven; his unswerving optimism; and for his passion, both for her, and for their life together.

This one is correct because the information before the colon is complete; it can stand on its own.

8   A   Never Eat Shredded Wheat: The Geography We've Lost and How to Find it Again

   B   Parisian Chic: A Style Guide

   c   Life and Laughing: My Story

D   Catherine of Aragon: Henry's Spanish Queen

E   Diary of a Wimpy Kid: Rodrick Rules

9   Only **B** should have a colon. **A** is too short and too informal to need one. **C** is interrupted mid-way by narrative information, and is only one sentence long anyway. In **D**, the speech is integrated into the sentence's syntax.

10   A   They are an odd couple; he is needy and she isn't.

B   He is not really a novelist in this respect; he is a proselytiser. (*Excellent! The world is rid of a comma splice.*)

C   It's a world away from chasing aliens, as we saw Anderson in *The X Files*; here she's a malevolent madam in Victorian London.

Neither **D** nor **E** can use a semicolon because the second part of each statement is an incomplete sentence. In the last example, the second half of the sentence cannot stand alone either; it is dependent on the first half to make sense of it.

11   A   Uh-oh. Things don't look good for Jen.

B   Sounds like they never got on as a couple. Perhaps he'd loathed her for years and this was his crowning moment. How stylish.

C   Hm, what's his dark secret? Or is he frightened that it's all too good to be true? No doubt all will become clear.

D   Billy was either heartbroken, or he was a bum who'd only been held together by marriage. Whichever is true, the divorce was the immediate cause of his downfall.

12   A   Jem was the product of their first year of marriage; four years later I was born, and two years later our mother died from a sudden heart attack.

B   Lastly, she packed up her books quickly, wrapping the most precious in clean, white tissue paper; for she couldn't bear to damage them.

13 **A** I don't really understand the fascination with cricket; however, I rather enjoy cucumber sandwiches and men in well-cut whites. / I don't really understand the fascination with cricket. However, I rather enjoy cucumber sandwiches and men in well-cut whites.

B He'd bought her a fantastic pair of shoes; nevertheless, he was still a two-timing pain in the ass. / He'd bought her a fantastic pair of shoes. Nevertheless, he was still a two-timing pain in the ass.

C She'd passed her final exams. Moreover, she'd managed it without losing her mind. / She'd passed her final exams; moreover, she'd managed it without losing her mind.

14 **A** The evening will run to the following sequence: embarrassing name badge distribution; awkward mingling; a welcome address; a champagne reception, requiring inane sniggering at each other's anxious jokes; a colourless speech by V G Copperplate, Ministry of Indecipherable Signatures; followed by a five course, silver service, gala dinner; and, thank God, carriages for midnight.

B We will need quite a few things: pens, plain black biros preferably; paper, white; a dictionary for Neil, who can't spell; a thesaurus for Clare, who lost her adult vocabulary while on maternity leave; a large, impressive desk; a whiteboard; markers; and, in case anyone gets hungry, a pizza menu.

C For a really good Knickerbocker Glory you must have ice cream, in three flavours if possible, fruit, cream, chopped nuts, chocolate sauce and a nice long spoon. (*The list items complete the sentence, so you cannot use a colon to start the list. Semicolons throughout would seem like overkill, though you may want to put one after 'possible'.*)

D The trainer had done everything he could with the mare: he had broken her in slowly with the most up-to-date techniques; he had hired skilled, gentle stable-hands, all of whom had come with impressive references; he had sought the help of animal psychologists, flying them in from Vienna and Munich; and yet, despite all, the bloody horse would not run.

Exercise 2

1   A   They had never seen a painting like it: murderous crows above a disturbingly animate cornfield.

   B   He loved her: she was everything he wanted.

   C   The beach was beautiful; above it, a single-track road rose into the valley.

   D   They wandered with no plans and without the pressures of time: even their talk was languid and unhurried.

   E   As a child I loved riding; I like the smell of hot horses and old leather.

2   In each case, the dash could be replaced with a semicolon. As with all semicolons, a valid option is also a full stop, since each sentence should be able to stand on its own:

   A   Chris's eyes sparkled. That's why Matt is such good casting; his eyes sparkle, too. / Chris's eyes sparkled. That's why Matt is such good casting. His eyes sparkle, too.

   B   The best thing about adulthood isn't owning a home or world travel; it's being able to buy your own snacks. / The best thing about adulthood isn't owning a home or world travel. It's being able to buy your own snacks.

   C   As usual, Toby is feeling ostracised. Well, of course he is; he's a loser. / As usual, Toby is feeling ostracised. Well, of course he is. He's a loser.

3   Here are the most sensible solutions, but you could create any number of fun combinations:

A   Lotte taught herself to play the guitar loudly; the couple next door were forgiving and tolerant.

B   Louisa was teased as a child in Bari; her red curls troubled her raven-haired peers.

C   Alice left the States for a new way of life; Paris and its romance beckoned her.

D   Samantha's biological clock was banging loudly in her ears; she was 38 with no boyfriend, never mind a husband.

E   Eleanor found a great job in the Embassy; she wasn't frightened of long hours or hard work.

Express Yourself: The Expressive Marks

Warm-up

1   No question marks are necessary since both are indirect questions.

2   The classic musical *High Society* includes unforgettable numbers like 'Well Did You Evah!' and 'Who Wants to be a Millionaire?' sung by a youthful Frank Sinatra.

Songs are not italicised, but the musical they appear in is. The same goes for songs on albums and CDs. They will usually be placed within quotation marks.

3   They arrived en masse though there was little room in the house. Some set up tents in the garden, and despite inclement weather, doggedly ate breakfast, lunch and supper *en plein air*.

'En masse' no longer needs italics as is it regarded as fully assimilated into the English language. (Those of you who are *Star Trek* fans will be striving to find a Borg joke in there!)

4   'And I said to him, "No Gavin, I will not take you back, no matter
    how many times you weep on the front doorstep till 4 a.m. singing
    Bryan Adams ballads. I never will." And when he heard that, he left
    for Amsterdam with that redhead from two doors down.'

5   You might have created something like this:

    Jeff (who hadn't seen his toes for a month) was feeling desperate
    about his weight gain.

Exercise 1

1 **A** 'Wow!' cried Baby Bear, 'Mum, dad! There's a cute blonde in my
       bed!'

   B 'And a natural one at that!' exclaimed Mummy Bear, admiringly.

2 **A** Daddy Bear gasped, 'Son, what in God's name have you been up
       to?'

   B Waking up into a full-blown domestic, Goldilocks wondered
       why on earth she'd thought breaking and entering was a good
       idea.

   C 'Why do you always have to jump to conclusions?' snapped
       Mummy Bear.

   D Watching her leave, Baby Bear asked himself what might have
       happened if he'd got her mobile number.

3 **A** Aretha Franklin's masterpiece *I Never Loved a Man the Way I Love
       You* is the album in which the Queen of Soul finds her voice.
       Tracks include ageless hits like 'Respect', 'Dr Feelgood' and 'Baby,
       Baby, Baby'.

   B An article on Macbeth called 'If Chance Would Have Me King'
       was published in *Fringe* magazine last month; it attracted both
       critical acclaim and controversy.

C First screened in 1986, 'Beer' was a particularly hilarious episode of the BBC TV series *Blackadder*, made even more memorable by Miriam Margolyes's aghast performance as Edmund's puritan aunt.

D Michelangelo's *David* is, undeniably, a fine figure of a man.

E Renoir's *Girl With a Watering Can* appeared in the Hollywood movies *Possessed* and *Lady in the Lake*, while Picasso's *The Lovers* can be spotted in the 1957 Hollywood musical, *Funny Face*.

F On April 17, 1975, Elvis bought a Convair 880 Jet and promptly named it the *Lisa Marie*. The *Belle of Louisville* is reputedly the oldest operating steamboat in the United States.

If you are surprised by **E** and **F** then it may be helpful to know that named ships, aircraft and vehicles should also be italicised. Don't confuse that with their model.

4 A They didn't have one, but *three* holidays a year.

B It's not the quantity that counts, but the *quality*.

C I can confidently state that your new boyfriend is *not* Elvis.

D It looks like a very handy gadget, but what does it *do*?

You may have been itching to italicise more than once in **A**, **B** and **D**. That's fine; it's your style, but remember that you can often achieve more with less.

5 A After reading about the destructive tendencies of *homo sapiens*, Eva felt she'd lost her *joie de vivre*.

B In the film *Dead Poets Society*, Robin Williams draws his students round a school photograph and exhorts them, sotto voce: '*Carpe diem*. Seize the day, boys. Make your lives extraordinary.'

C The lecturer droned on ad nauseum; Jamie committed the terrible faux pas of falling asleep in the front row during a televised lecture.

D   It was a *fait accompli* that Jamie's snooze would be caught on camera. Amongst the tutors of the University's *ancien régime*, he came to be seen as something of a *bête noire*.

E   'Well,' muttered Jamie en route home from his worst tutorial yet, '*c'est la vie.*'

This is an unfair test as it is notoriously difficult to know what is classed as 'assimilated' and what is not. However, it does at least demonstrate that italicising foreign words and phrases is a tricky business and is changing all the time. The best rule of thumb is to check in an up-to-date dictionary or, failing that, err on the side of caution by italicising.

6   A   People seem to get terribly confused by *there*, *their*, and *they're*. I've never understood why.

B   Shouldn't we start a campaign to resurrect fabulous words that have fallen out of favour? On my list would be gems like *ramshackle*, *ragamuffin* and – the incomparable – *swizz*.

C   I still have to count out every *s*, every *i*, and every *p* in *Mississippi*, in the same way I have to say the letters of the alphabet out loud when I use a dictionary. It's slightly worrying.

D   When it comes to computing, what is the plural of *mouse*?

7   A   'I wonder', he murmured, touching her cheek, 'whether I might possibly come up for coffee?'

B   'Excuse me mister,' she spat, hands on ample hips, 'I ain't that kind of girl.'

Note the first comma working differently in **A** and **B**. That's because in **B**, the speaker will have paused after the first phrase, so the comma comes inside the quotation marks; she does actually 'say' it.

C   'Do you know what he said to me? He said, "Janice, I don't love you anymore." So I belted him. Who the hell is Janice?'

If you resisted the urge to put an exclamation mark on 'So I belted him,' then I salute you; less is undeniably more when it comes to expressive punctuation.

8 A Why is it that, since 1977, I can only think of Luke Skywalker trying to blow up a Death Star when I hear the simple words 'almost there'?

   B Was there ever a better understatement than 'Houston, we have a problem'?

   C He seemed surprised when she gasped: 'I haven't seen you for a year and then you turn up out of the blue and ask me what's for dinner. Who the hell do you think you are?'

9 In each case, either paired dashes or round brackets are appropriate, though they will create subtle differences in effect. Both of these options are actually more fitting than the commas used in the examples.

10 A Emma Harding (who had never been inside an aeroplane until a month ago) fulfilled her lifelong ambition today when she gained her pilot's licence today.

    B Her children Luke (8) and Matilda (12) were present at her first (admittedly erratic) unaccompanied flight.

    C Interviewed later, the children described how proud they were of their determined (though sometimes unpredictable) mother.

You could imagine that, if covered in a tabloid, this story might have been printed with dashes to exclaim Emma's eccentricities. In a broadsheet, the bracket might be used to downplay her failings. Real life is not so simplistic, but you can see the potential distinction.

11 Some examples:

    A He was young, stylish, and wealthy (the lucky blighter). Owner of an Aston Martin and 400 acres, and husband to a stunning blonde, he had every reason (you betcha!) to be content in life.

B J. Lo has always claimed (over and over and over) she's still Jenny from the block.

Yours will be completely different, and much better. Basically anything that doesn't disrupt the meaning of the host sentence, but that adds to it, or undermines it, is acceptable.

12 **A** Their argument endured from dawn until dusk. (For their tempestuous relationship, this was not unusual.)

B Their argument endured from dawn until dusk (and was not unusual).

13 **A** In *On the Waterfront,* Marlon Brandow [sic] was unforgettable as Terry Malloy, brooding misfit of the New York Docks.

B Really Dull Street [sic] in Fresno was featured in a CBS news report about unbelievable place names.

14 **A** His ignorance was as remarkable as his knowledge ... That any civilised human being in this nineteenth century should not be aware that the earth travelled round the sun appeared to be to me such an extraordinary fact that I could scarcely realise it.

B In April 2010 a woman was banned from entering Disneyland Paris because she was dressed as a princess ... she was told by staff that her costume might 'confuse' the children.

You may have chosen to cut a different portion, or may have cut the same area earlier or later. Anything goes, as long as you have 'cut to the chase' of what was said.

15 **A** The question of whether computers will ever develop intuition throws up more interesting science and deep ideas than you might expect: the excellent Dr Hal Sinclair investigates ...

B They'd shared a simple picnic in Central Park, sat close in a matinee movie, and held hands on the breezy top of the Empire

State Building. Touching her hair as they waited in Grand Central Station, Tom asked haltingly if Marcy would like to come back to his place ...

Exercise 2

1 A 'You will never have the balls to ask her out,' said Robin.

   B Nick set down his drink dejectedly and replied, 'I'll prove you wrong. I just need the right moment.'

   C 'Man, I don't mean to be funny, but you've been saying that for 18 months; you haven't got what it takes.'

   D *No change*: Nick had always found 'I don't mean to be funny' to be a particularly ludicrous and offensive phrase.

2 A UK

   B US/Canada

3 A Never was a line more convincingly delivered by a child actor than Haley Joel Osment's 'I see dead people.'

   B After slaving in a grimy diner for three years to fund his thesis, Marvin folded his apron and swore, 'I will never touch mayonnaise again.'

   C Ed was nonplussed by her reaction to his well-meaning compliment that she was 'probably the second prettiest girl at the party'.

When Words Collide: The Hyphen

Warm-up

1 A She finally decided to end their long-doomed relationship.

   B Heartbroken, he took solace in ordering an extra-large pizza.

2   A   He was pretty easy on the eye for a balding sixty-two-year-old.

    B   It's said that only two-thirds of Americans own a passport.

3   If you use a dash to denote range, you must never use *from* at the same time. If you use *from*, you should express the range like this:

    Dinner is served from 18.00 to 22.00.

4   A   The demands of his high-maintenance wife were making him feel progressively run down.

    B   His hard-pressed secretary couldn't fathom why her boss was suddenly so worn out too.

5   A   Yes, a hyphen is always needed when a prefix appears before a capitalised proper name.

    B   Yes, a hyphen is always needed when a prefix appears before a capitalised proper name.

    C   Yes, a hyphen is always required when a prefix appears before a numeral or date.

6   A   He had expertly de-emphasised his part in the stag night fracas.

    B   She was now co-owner of a new, sleek and rather enticing pink yacht.

7   A   London was a melting pot; upper-, middle- and lower-class citizens mingled in its unhygienic streets.

    B   She loved the design so much, she bought twelve first- and six second-class Christmas stamps.

Exercise 1

1   A   She re-dressed the catwalk volunteers under the watchful gaze of her terrifying boss.

    B   The re-formation has had global consequences. Everyone is coming to terms with the fact that Take That are getting on a bit.

C   After her favourite student was found cheating, Jess had to re-mark every paper.

D   Katie re-served the gateau after a couple of hours when they had room to eat it.

E   After protracted — but successful — contract negotiations, the infamous TV presenter finally re-signed.

F   She had never re-covered a cushion in that way before. But, by golly, there was a first time for everything.

2 A   Harry made a pre-emptive strike for the first slice of chocolate gateau.

B   Emily was nervous about turning up on time for her pre-op.

C   The red squirrel has been largely ousted by the non-native grey.

D   It is never easy to work part-time.

E   The honeymoon destination was non-negotiable: Las Vegas or bust.

F   A word you hear less and less is *slap-happy*. If only it were true of the trait.

G   The letter on her doormat looked semi-official and a bit threatening.

H   The second-rate thriller they had wasted good money on seeing was, well, thrill-less.

I   One word of encouragement and she was re-energised for a week.

3 A   In the ballroom's Lost and Found, Dorothy found an exquisite pair of long-forgotten dress gloves.

B   Arriving nervously at the Halloween party, Matt was faced by forty-odd people drinking blood-red punch.

C   As a trusted security guard at an exclusive New York hotel, he'd enjoyed a long-standing career.

D A renowned penny-pincher, Molly always kept a second-hand towel in her bathroom.

E Always prepared, her twin sister Milly always kept a second hand-towel in her bathroom.

F Graham eased himself comfortably into the first-class seat he'd spotted that morning.

G As a 40th birthday treat, she'd decided to buy herself an extra-fast sports car.

H Livid with his wayward wife, Mike began his cross-questioning over the barbecue.

I Two foot-soldiers were found outrageously drunk while on duty.

The last example is an interesting one since foot soldiers would not normally take a hyphen. However, in this ambiguous context it would probably be prudent to use one to clarify the meaning.

4 A Will you still need me, will you still feed me, when I'm sixty-four?

B Never one to miss good publicity, he gave away two-thirds of his footballing salary on his twenty-first birthday.

C The fifty-five-year-old broadcaster can still turn the heads of adoring twenty-somethings.

D The thirty-year-old British male is often motivated by the pursuit of curry.

5 A is correct.

B is not correct: the gap on either side of the dash should be closed.

C is correct.

D is correct.

E is not correct: never use *from* with a dash that denotes range.

6 **A** two people

B one (very bad actor)

C two

7 **A** Her job was high profile, so she chose to date only high-powered men.

B *No change*: Sara was completely disorganised; she hadn't had time to top up her phone or set up a new bank account.

C Miles had stupidly hired a highly strung secretary with a waif-like figure and a penchant for rice cakes.

D Richard had made a well-timed proposal. His rose-tinted day-dreams saw them as a happily married couple, while his realist streak fretted that Tamsin may require some extra-marital thrills.

E He came from a built-up area rife with crime; nevertheless he'd built up quite a reputation as a nice guy who helped old ladies across the street.

F Our newly designed anti-ageing cream will reduce laugh-line creasing and minimise even deep-set wrinkles.

G The film had an irresistible feel-good factor.

8 **A** I) pro-Clinton

B I) Proto-Germanic and III) protolanguage

C II) antimatter

D II) antibacterial and III) antibiotics

E II) quasi-scientific

F III) Seventh-Day Adventists

9 **A** Just one, before *women*, to denote that they too are *countrywomen*.

B Three: *first-, second- and third-rate movies*.

C Just two: *ten-, a hundred-, a thousandfold.*

D Two: *He bought both the single- and the double-breasted suit.*

E Three: *Italian-, French- and English-speaking family.*

F Two: *blue- and white-collar workers.*

Exercise 2

1 A Yes, always. Regardless of position, you should always hyphenate the suffixes *-like* and *-less* if they immediately follow two *l*s in the preceding word.

B No: *moonscape* is an accepted form.

C No: *ladylike* is a well-established form that traditionally does not need a hyphen.

D Yes: hyphenate here because the suffix butts up against two capitals, in the same way that you would hyphenate a prefix before a capital, e.g. anti-Darwinian.

E No: *snowscape* is established enough not to require a hyphen.

F Yes: err on the side of caution as this is a more rarely heard form.

G No: *bulletproof* is an accepted form.

H Yes: probably best to err on the side of caution with this one. Keep checking up-to-date dictionaries however, as the hyphen may be officially ditched.

I Yes: this is a very specific use and should be hyphenated.

J No: *lengthwise* is a long-established form.

K No: *splashproof* is a fairly accepted form.

L No: *otherwise* is a long-established form.

M Yes: this is a personal and specific use. Further, this use of the suffix, where it is added on to a noun to mean 'as regards to' is an informal and (in punctuation terms at least) fairly new development. It will become more common however, so keep your eye on recent dictionaries.

2 A For the big-screen adaptation he had to play a judge whose demeanour was constantly heavy-hearted.

B The large-scale production was often hindered by the tantrums of the director who was bad-tempered.

C Thankfully the award-winning producer was calm and clear-sighted.

D It was a big break for the hard-up lead actor: always quick-witted and affable.

E As a peak-time drama it should work; everyone loves a period piece set in the 19th century.

F Whatever happened, the final cut would be thought-provoking.

If you decided not to use a hyphen in the last example, you are still correct but the meaning will be quite different. Without the hyphen, whatever happened, the final cut would be thought *to be* provoking.

3 A Impressionism dominated French art in the late nineteenth century.

B Finally, older women can enjoy the confidence of skin that is free of age spots.

C The former editor-in-chief was a grumpy man with a bulging waistline and an ego to match.

The Challenge

1 A New boy band suffers hearing loss from girls' screaming.

B Owner of a successful events management company, Chris Cairns organises parties and functions, whatever your budget.

c   Daisies just in. Perfect for a summer wedding.

d   It was ending: the affair that destroyed his marriage.

e   Free-range hen chicks: please mind your step.

f   Any one of these could work. Normal grammar considerations fall away a little when advertising:

For rent: secluded holiday cottage – perfect for couples – with stunning views.

For rent: secluded holiday cottage, perfect for couples; with stunning views.

For rent: secluded holiday cottage, perfect for couples, with stunning views.

For rent: secluded holiday cottage, perfect for couples. With stunning views.

g   Don't panic: breathe deeply, or swig a large brandy.

2   In December 2009 I went to see *Sorcery: The Legend* in 3D; I was blown away as it immersed me into its fictional world completely.

I received my copy of the Collector's edition earlier this week and have just watched it. This re-released, three-disc version contains the original cut, a previous re-release version and seventeen minutes' added footage. This footage does flesh out some of the characters and adds more of a background including a brilliantly added opening sequence with the much-awaited, high-speed broomstick chase.

Although the extras are a bonus I am, however, disappointed. The film has been cut into two sections, which means you have to change DVDs halfway through to continue viewing. Why couldn't the creators put the film on one DVD, thus enhancing the viewing experience? What their thinking is behind this split eludes me completely; it's very annoying.

The added material on this Collector's DVD is *some* compensation for the break halfway; I couldn't help but feel let down, though, as a lot of the extras mentioned on their advertisements are not included in the non-Blu-ray version that I bought. Note to distributors: people who don't have Blu-ray aren't second-class citizens.

If you're a fan of the film you will still enjoy the Collector's edition, despite its flaws.

3   The wind howled. Aged sixteen, away from home for his first lads' holiday, and secretly pining for the safety of his own bedroom, Owen was terrified; he just couldn't let on that he was. Balanced precariously on an exposed, remote hilltop overlooking the sea, their big, decrepit – and therefore cheap – caravan shook every night. Of his five friends, he found that the boys who had been away before were faring best. Admittedly, however, it was clear they were all miserable. The wind shrieked on. It was an unrelenting wind, an alarming wind, a wind that tore at their hair; it was a thief, a trickster, a mischievous imp snatching repeatedly at their over-optimistic holiday clothes and driving sharp rain into their eyes. The boys avoided eye contact; all jokes were self-consciously upbeat. Every last pretty girl had fled from the beleaguered resort now: sandblasting was rough on their luminous complexions. God, it was soul destroying; nevertheless, he was determined to stick the holiday – if you could call it that – out. Those of the group who had crueller natures waited smugly for him to bail out: he would not. 'No way,' he muttered. 'Not in a million years.'

4   In the summer of '85 Susannah had been a smart, beautiful girl with a bright future; in the autumn of '94 she was a world-weary housewife who today – without a second's guilt – had removed her cut-price wedding ring for good.

Wearing a figure-hugging dress that she'd bought only last week (with money Greg had grudgingly given her to buy a new vacuum cleaner), Susannah snapped shut her faux-leather suitcase, ran her eyes once round the ill-fated bedroom and made for the door. Hollering brightly for Sam and Louisa, she scurried down the stairs like a flushed, hopeful teenager on a first date.

Downstairs, after buttoning up the kids' coats, she stopped only to rescue one further thing: her copy of *It's a Wonderful Life* had long languished on Greg's tightly packed shelf of second-rate horror movies.

In only twenty-five minutes' time she, Sam and Louisa would be on the Washington–New York–Boston line to join the friends and family she had mistakenly left behind: to a new, well-furnished house they would call home; to a secure job with great prospects; to the care and support of friends, both hers and the children's; to laughter, safety and happiness; to a life without Greg O'Keeffe. Perhaps Susannah might also find the one thing that had eluded her for nine wasted years: love.

5   'Hey! They're back. They're coming this way!' cried Rob.

Head in hands, Matt mumbled, 'Good grief, we're in trouble now.'

'She's brought reinforcements. There are three – no four – more of them,' wailed Harry.

Who would have believed that a pretty – though troublesome – brunette would wreak such havoc for the sake of one ill-advised, stag weekend kiss.

'Quick! We've got to hide!' spluttered Rob.

'Where in God's name are we going to hide?' groaned Matt, 'It's a beach, for Pete's sake!'

'Hang on – surely not – who's that with them?' stumbled Rob, 'Uh-oh, is it? No, it couldn't – but it looks just like – is it? It can't be!'

'Yes, it is. It's my future father-in-law,' gasped Harry. 'Well, guys, it's been a blast, but I'm out of here!' As he scarpered, barefoot and sunburned, down the scalding white sand, the boys could just hear him shout 'See you at the wedding – if there is one!'

6   The foursome had put together a sumptuous picnic for their al fresco day lazing in Hyde Park. After bickering in nearby delis, they had acquired a feast *par excellence*: two bottles of good red wine; rye bread, just baked; three pungent cheeses; olives; potato salad; hand-cooked crisps crusted with sea salt; four glossy pastries; fresh cherries; cashews – dry-roasted of course; a large slab of very dark chocolate; and one Gingham tablecloth. Natalie started with the olives; Rose, the cashews; Ned and Marcus, the red wine.

Before long, conversation turned to (what they believed to be) lucid observations about life; it was always the same when wine was involved. Ned remarked that there was one thing that always disappointed him about picnics: lying on your stomach was never as comfortable as you expect. Marcus observed that there was a fairly effective solution to that: lying on your back. The girls opted out of the boys' nonsensical sparring; it was often the wisest course of action. Natalie stuck her attractive nose into Bill Bryson's *At Home: A Short History of Private Life*, since having a home and an intimate, normal private life instead of bumming about with a non-committal boyfriend was something for which she dearly wished. The previous year had been her *annus horribilis*: Marcus had bought her a Wii Fit – rather than a hoped-for solitaire – on her twenty-ninth birthday. It was a painful insight into his priorities, and had taken some time to get over. In calculated retribution, she had forced him to spend Christmas at her parents' house, *en famille*. It was a satisfying, if temporary, revenge.

Rose's plans for the future were very different to Natalie's: Ned didn't figure in them. She had often wondered why the heck she had wasted so much time on him. Goodness, the guy could be an idiot. Recently, she had looked up a former boyfriend – just for old times' sake – and found that after one clandestine *caffè latte* with him, she was re-evaluating everything about her relationship with Ned. There was no doubt about it: Ned was for the boot.

7   The newsroom of the *Weekly Tribune* (and its hastily written supplements) was a frenetic, squalid and somewhat smelly place. Rich had, until recently, kept asking himself why he had ever wanted

a job there. What had made it seem like such a good idea at the time? Perhaps Rich, accident-prone, shy and blighted with a stammer from childhood, was trying to prove something to himself or (as was far more likely) to his unfeeling parents.

He shared a desk with a neurotic and under-fed girl called Isobel. Isobel invariably looked as if she were badly in want of a meal, and seemed to survive joylessly on coffee, pre-sliced fruit trays and Marlboro Lights. Surprisingly, given her job title of Features Editor, Isobel had a problem with even basic spelling and was continuously double-checking with Rich rather than open a dictionary herself. His stammer often made such exchanges a little problematic:

'Rich! *Recommend.* Spell it for me?'

'R-E-C-C-C-O-M-M-M-E-N-D.'

'Never! Goodness, three of each?'

'No, I m-m-mean—'

'Great, Rich, thanks; you're the best.'

Never having the time to wait for his hesitant explanations, Isobel would charge on recklessly, only to suffer the inevitable wrath of the *Tribune*'s short-tempered editor, Joe Jones – JJ to both friends and enemies – who fancied himself as the all-powerful boss in Lou Grant. JJ even wore braces to underline the likeness (which ended there) and was doggedly working on attaining the fictional newsman's girth with a diet of glazed doughnuts, take-out pizzas and full-calorie Cokes. He was nauseating: Rich loathed him, not only for his greasy-faced smugness, but for the vindictive way in which he ridiculed his journalists' offerings, especially Isobel's. For Rich was coming to realise one all-important and assertive fact in his otherwise halting existence: Isobel was the one.

8   Police arrested a man yesterday on suspicion of being repeatedly drunk and disorderly in charge of a horse. Arthur Brown (57) of Ross-shire was spotted on several different occasions riding his

seven-year-old grey mare, Lusitania, while apparently under the influence of alcohol. Local housewife and eyewitness Annie Keenan said: 'You could see [Arthur] riding down the High Street nearly every day, barely staying on that poor animal. The beast just kept plodding towards home with Arthur swaying from side to side and hauling himself back up with the reins, singing at the top of his voice the whole time. His feet kept slipping out of them stirrups [sic] too, and he'd have to shimmy about until he got them back in. Shocking, it is, although that lovely mare doesn't seem to mind at all.'

Brown, a local councillor, stated that he had 'never touched a drop' while riding and that his eccentric style of horsemanship was instead 'a new technique [he had] learned from Mortimer Drinkup [sic].' Mr Drinkup, an ex-horse-whisperer who now organises combined riding and whisky-tasting holidays in New England, was unavailable for comment.

9 Martha had discovered the joy of reading as a small child, through some rather inappropriate texts. Her parents – marriage counsellors as well as overworked doctors – had a large white cupboard in their bedroom, in which resided every book on marital discord ever written. These works contained details, not only of the argumentative perils of finance, division of duties, and conflicting expectations, but revelations of a more intimate kind, ranging from couples with mismatched pre- and post-nuptial appetites to some rather bewildering deviances which made Martha first wince, then re-read the relevant passages fascinatedly. After Martha volunteered a few startling terms from her impressive new vocabulary at a parish fundraiser, declaring brightly that she'd 'learned them from Mummy and Daddy's special books', the cupboard was never left unlocked again.

So began her fascination with words, albeit from an inauspicious start. A self-sufficient and often remote child, she graduated quickly from *Danny the Champion of the World* and *Charlotte's Web* to darker tales that indulged her obsession with language. *The Phantom Tolbooth* (peopled with marketeers selling pronouns by the pound) was first to truly absorb her, followed swiftly by

Alice in Wonderland's stumblings into the lifeblood of semantics. Ray Bradbury's 'A Sound of Thunder' – in which one crushed butterfly changes the course of human and linguistic history – was the short story she held responsible for her study of English Language at university.

In later life, she'd heard tell of a website from which one could 'purchase' words for charity. She blew three months' wages on *chiaroscuro*, *luminescence*, *quinquereme* and *opsimath*, before framing them – expensively – for her study. Having run out of cash, she asked her husband sweetly if he'd buy *serenity* for her forty-second birthday. He agreed, throwing in *devotion* for good luck.

References

Who Do You Think You Are?

[1] Terry Pratchett *Mort*

At Your Service, Master: The Apostrophe

[1] George Eliot
[2] Lewis Carroll *Through the Looking Glass*
[3] Charles Dickens *The Pickwick Papers*
[4] Mark Twain *The Adventures of Huckleberry Finn*
[5] Jerome K Jerome *Three Men in a Boat*
[6] From the Apostrophe Protection Society
[7] From the Apostrophe Protection Society
[8] Lord Camrose (1879–1954)
[9] Jerome K Jerome *Three Men in a Boat*
[10] Henry Ford (1863–1947)
[11] Charles Dickens *A Christmas Carol*
[12] Michel Faber *The Crimson Petal and the White*

Catch My Meaning? Catch Your Breath: The Comma

[1] Edmund Blackadder *Blackadder Goes Forth*
[2] Philip Snowden (1864–1937)
[3] Charles Dickens *Sketches by Boz*
[4] Lewis Carroll *Alice in Wonderland*
[5] Lewis Carroll *Alice in Wonderland*
[6] Walter Bagehot (1826–1877)
[7] PG Wodehouse *My Man Jeeves*
[8] John Train, ed. *Wit: The Best Things Ever Said*
[9] Alan Bennett *Beyond the Fringe*
[10] Zelda Fitzgerald (1900–1948)
[11] Barbara Walraff *Word Court*
[12] Jack Kerouac *On the Road*
[13] Ronald Firbank (1886–1926)
[14] *Radio Times* 26 March–1 April 2011

References

A Theatrical Flourish: The Colon and Semicolon

[1] Jerome K Jerome *Three Men in a Boat*

[2] O. Henry (William Sidney Porter; 1862–1910)

[3] George Bernard Shaw *Arms and the Man*

[4] G. M. Young (1882–1959)

[5] Harper Lee *To Kill a Mockingbird*

[6] Winston Churchill (1874–1965) (of Viscount Montgomery)

[7] Excerpt from the Monty Python 'Argument Clinic' sketch. From David Crystal *Language Play*

[8] Richard Brautigan *Revenge of the Lawn*

[9] Benjamin Disraeli (1804–1881)

[10] Tennessee Williams (1911–1983)

[11] Harper Lee *To Kill A Mockingbird*

[12] Evelyn Waugh *Brideshead Revisited*

[13] *Radio Times* 19–25 March 2011

[14] Charles Dickens *Nicholas Nickleby*

[15] Harper Lee *To Kill a Mockingbird*

[16] *Radio Times* 19–25 March 2011

Express Yourself: The Expressive Marks

[1] William Shakespeare *Romeo and Juliet*

[2] Charles Dickens *A Christmas Carol*

[3] Lewis Carroll *Alice in Wonderland*

[4] Jane Austen *Sense and Sensibility*

[5] Nancy Astor (1879–1964)

[6] Charles Dickens *Nicholas Nickleby*

[7] Jane Austen *Sense and Sensibility*

[8] Arthur Conan Doyle *A Study in Scarlet*

When Words Collide: The Hyphen

[1] *The Cannonball Run* (1981)

This title uses the *Collins English Dictionary (10ᵗʰ Edition)* as its source of reference.

Lightning Source UK Ltd.
Milton Keynes UK
UKOW01f2339120218

317771UK00002B/213/P